Fast food VEGAN

First Edition: 2023

Published by Taste of Vegan

Printed in USA

The recipes, techniques, and tips in this cookbook are intended for personal use only. The author and publisher are not responsible for any adverse effects or consequences resulting from the use of the recipes or suggestions in this book.

Library of Congress Cataloging-in-Publication Data:

First edition.
Includes index.

Manufactured in USA

Introduction

Ladies and gentlemen, fellow food adventurers, and lovers of all things delicious, I extend to you a warm and hearty welcome to the Fast Food Vegan Cookbook: Satisfy Cravings, Stay Vegan. In these pages, we're embarking on a culinary journey that might just challenge everything you thought you knew about fast food.

Now, you might be wondering, "Vegan and fast food? Can those two worlds truly collide in a way that satisfies cravings and keeps us on the plant-based path?" My answer is a resounding "Yes!" The theme of this cookbook is simple yet groundbreaking: we're here to bring the thrill of fast food into the realm of vegan living.

You see, my inspiration for creating this cookbook stemmed from a desire to show the world that veganism is not about deprivation; it's about creativity and indulgence. It's about celebrating the flavors, textures, and excitement of fast food while remaining true to our plant-based principles. It's about proving that you can have your vegan burger and eat it too.

What can you expect to find within these pages? Well, my friends, prepare yourselves for a tantalizing array of 100+ plant-based, fast food-inspired recipes that will satisfy your cravings without compromising your commitment to veganism. From mouthwatering burgers that'll make your taste buds sing to crispy, golden fries that redefine the art of snacking, we've got it all covered.

But this isn't just about replicating fast food favorites; it's about elevating them. We're diving into the world of sauces, seasonings, and creative combinations to ensure that every bite is an adventure. And fear not, for we've included pictures to tantalize your senses and guide you on this culinary expedition.

So, fasten your seatbelts and prepare to embark on a fast food journey like no other. In the pages that follow, you'll discover the secrets of creating vegan versions of iconic fast food classics. It's a celebration of bold flavors, indulgent textures, and the belief that being vegan doesn't mean giving up on the pleasure of fast food.

I hope you're hungry because we're about to redefine what it means to satisfy those cravings while staying firmly rooted in the world of plant-based living. So grab your apron, fire up the stove, and let's get cooking, fast food style—with a vegan twist.

Vegan Teriyaki Bowl

See page, 50

Cooking Philosophy or Approach

In the world of fast food, where sizzling burgers and crispy fries often reign supreme, I invite you to explore a new frontier—a realm where flavor knows no bounds, and veganism takes center stage. Welcome to the Fast Food Vegan Cookbook: Satisfy Cravings, Stay Vegan, where we've crafted over 100 plant-based recipes inspired by the indulgent world of fast food.

My approach to cooking and food in this cookbook is rooted in the belief that eating vegan doesn't mean sacrificing taste or convenience. It's about transforming familiar fast-food favorites into wholesome, plant-powered delights that will satisfy even the most insatiable cravings.

In our culinary journey, we'll harness the magic of whole food ingredients and innovative techniques to replicate the textures and flavors that fast food aficionados know and love. We'll explore the versatility of plant-based proteins like tempeh, seitan, and tofu, crafting them into mouthwatering burgers, crispy nuggets, and succulent kebabs.

Our sauces and condiments will transport you to the heart of flavor, with homemade vegan mayo, tangy barbecue sauces, and creamy dairy-free dressings that are every bit as satisfying as their traditional counterparts. And don't worry; we'll share the secrets to achieving that perfect balance of savory, sweet, and umami that defines fast-food fare.

But it's not just about replicating the classics. We'll also embark on a journey of culinary innovation, introducing you to exciting, globally inspired creations that will keep your taste buds constantly intrigued. From spicy Korean-inspired tofu tacos to hearty Mediterranean-style falafel wraps, we'll prove that vegan fast food can be as diverse as it is delicious.

In this cookbook, you'll find step-by-step instructions accompanied by vibrant pictures, ensuring that each dish is not only mouthwatering but also accessible to even the most novice home cook. Whether you're a seasoned vegan or just starting on your plant-based journey, you'll discover that fast food can be both guilt-free and utterly irresistible.

So, join me as we redefine fast food—where every bite is a celebration of flavor, compassion, and the joy of staying true to your vegan values. It's a culinary adventure that will keep you craving more and, most importantly, keep you firmly on the path to a vegan lifestyle.

Vegan Tacos al Pastor
See page, 37

Tips for Successful Cooking

Alright, folks, welcome to the Fast Food Vegan Cookbook, where we're about to unleash a whirlwind of flavor without compromising on our commitment to staying vegan. In these pages, you'll find over 100 plant-based, fast-food-inspired recipes that will make your taste buds dance and your conscience clear.

But before we dive headfirst into the culinary chaos, let's talk shop—cooking shop, that is. Here are some tips and techniques to ensure you navigate this vegan fast-food adventure with skill and gusto:

1. Fresh is Best: Start with the freshest ingredients you can find. Whether it's veggies, fruits, or tofu, the quality of your ingredients will shine through in the final dish.

2. Knife Skills: Get comfortable with that chef's knife. A sharp blade is your best friend in the kitchen. Proper chopping and slicing not only make your prep work faster but also ensure even cooking.

3. Seasoning Savvy: Don't be shy with the spices. Vegan food can explode with flavor when you master the art of seasoning. Experiment with herbs, spices, and condiments to create depth and character in your dishes.

4. Texture Matters: Pay attention to the texture of your ingredients. Achieving the right balance of crunch and tenderness can take your dish from good to unforgettable. Think about how different textures complement each other.

5. Balance the Flavors: Balancing flavors is key. Think sweet, salty, sour, and spicy. Adjust as needed to achieve the perfect harmony in your dishes.

6. Master the Heat: Understand your stovetop or oven. Each appliance has its quirks, and knowing how to control the heat is essential for precise cooking.

7. Experiment and Innovate: Fast food is all about experimentation. Don't be afraid to put your own spin on these recipes. Add a unique sauce or toss in a surprise ingredient—make it your own.

8. Timing is Everything: Pay attention to cooking times. Overcooking can turn even the best ingredients into a culinary disaster. Keep an eye on the clock, but don't be a slave to it either. Sometimes a little extra time can turn a good dish into an exceptional one.

9. Plating Prowess: Presentation matters, even in fast food. Take a moment to plate your dishes attractively. A well-presented meal is not only more appealing but also more satisfying.

10. Practice Makes Perfect: Lastly, remember that like any skill, cooking gets better with practice. Don't be discouraged by the occasional mishap; it's all part of the journey. Learn, adapt, and most importantly, enjoy the process.

As you embark on your fast-food-inspired vegan cooking adventure, keep these tips in mind. They'll be your trusty companions in the kitchen, ensuring that every dish you whip up from this cookbook is a tantalizing, vegan triumph. So let's get cooking, my fellow plant-based food adventurers, and let's savor every delicious moment along the way.

Vegan Mac and Cheese
See page, 27

Kitchen Essentials

Alright, folks, before we dive headfirst into the mouthwatering world of fast food-inspired vegan cuisine, let's talk about the tools of the trade. Just like a great chef relies on their trusty knives and seasoned skillet, you'll want to have a few essential kitchen gadgets at your disposal to conquer these 100+ plant-based fast food recipes.

Kitchen Essentials:

1. High-Speed Blender: This is your ticket to silky-smooth vegan milkshakes, creamy sauces, and luscious smoothie bowls. Don't skimp on quality; invest in a good one.

2. Cast Iron Skillet: Your best friend for achieving that perfect sear on plant-based burgers and crispy tofu. It's versatile, sturdy, and will last a lifetime with proper care.

3. Food Processor: For finely chopping, dicing, and mincing ingredients like onions, garlic, and nuts. It's also your secret weapon for making vegan "meat" crumbles.

4. Quality Chef's Knife: A sharp knife is a chef's most important tool. It makes chopping veggies and slicing through ingredients like a breeze. Keep it honed and ready.

5. Non-Stick Baking Sheet: Ideal for roasting vegetables, baking vegan pastries, or creating crispy fries without excessive oil.

6. Vegetable Spiralizer: For turning zucchinis into noodles and other veggies into fun shapes for salads and garnishes.

7. Citrus Juicer: Fresh lemon and lime juice add zing to your dishes. A handheld juicer makes extracting that liquid gold a breeze.

8. Silicone Baking Mats: Perfect for baking without sticking and reducing the need for parchment paper or excessive oil.

Tips on How to Use These Tools Effectively:

Keep Your Blades Sharp: A dull knife is a dangerous knife. Invest in a quality knife sharpener and hone your skills to keep your knives in top condition.

Master the Blender: Learn how to layer ingredients properly in your blender for smoothies, starting with liquids, followed by soft and hard ingredients. Blend in stages, and don't overfill.

Cast Iron Care: Season your cast iron skillet properly to create a non-stick surface. After cooking, clean it with hot water and a brush (no soap!), then dry it thoroughly and lightly oil it.

Food Processor Precision: Pulse your food processor for better control over the texture of ingredients. It's your secret weapon for achieving the right consistency in vegan burger patties, dips, and spreads.

Use Your Citrus Juicer Efficiently: Cut citrus fruits in half crosswise to make juicing more manageable. Roll them gently on the counter before juicing to release more juice.

Keep Your Baking Sheets Clean: Line your baking sheets with silicone baking mats or parchment paper to make cleanup easier, especially when roasting veggies or baking.

Remember, a chef is only as good as their tools, so make sure you're well-equipped to tackle these fast food-inspired vegan creations. With the right gear and a bit of culinary finesse, you'll be whipping up plant-based fast food feasts in no time. So, get ready to satisfy those cravings and stay true to your vegan lifestyle!

Flavor Pairing Suggestions

Alright, my fellow culinary adventurers, let's dive into the exciting realm of flavor pairing in the Fast Food Vegan Cookbook. In the world of fast food-inspired, plant-based cuisine, it's not just about following recipes; it's about unleashing your creativity, experimenting, and discovering new flavor combinations that will tantalize your taste buds.

Here are some tantalizing ideas for complementary flavors and ingredients that can serve as your passport to crafting unique and delectable fast food vegan creations:

1. Sweet and Savory Harmony: One of the classic pairings that never fails to please is the combination of sweet and savory. Think of drizzling maple syrup over crispy tempeh bacon or adding pineapple to your vegan burger for a burst of sweetness against the savory backdrop.

2. Heat and Sweet: Spice things up with a touch of heat paired with a hint of sweetness. Try adding jalapeño slices to your BBQ pulled jackfruit sandwich, or infuse your vegan chili with a touch of agave nectar to balance the fire.

3. Creamy and Crunchy: Texture plays a significant role in the world of flavors. Combine creamy avocado with crispy fried chickpeas in your tacos, or dollop cashew-based ranch dressing onto a crunchy vegan Buffalo cauliflower wing.

4. Fresh and Tangy: Elevate your dishes with freshness and tanginess. Toss a handful of arugula with lemon vinaigrette to brighten up your vegan Caesar salad, or top your vegan hot dog with sauerkraut for that classic tang.

5. Umami Explosion: Embrace umami by adding ingredients like shiitake mushrooms or miso paste to your dishes. They bring depth and savoriness that can make your vegan ramen or stir-fry unforgettable.

6. Herbs and Citrus: Fresh herbs and citrus zest can take your flavors to a whole new level. Sprinkle chopped cilantro and a squeeze of lime onto your vegan tacos or zest up your tofu scramble with lemon.

7. Nuts and Berries: For a touch of earthy richness and natural sweetness, try incorporating crushed nuts and fresh berries into your fast food-inspired vegan bowls or desserts.

8. Global Fusion: Get adventurous by fusing flavors from different cuisines. Add curry powder to your sweet potato fries, or blend Mexican spices into your vegan sushi rolls.

Remember, my friends, these are just a few starting points. The world of flavor is vast, and your palate is your canvas. Don't hesitate to experiment, take risks, and create your own signature fast food vegan masterpieces. Whether you're satisfying cravings or staying vegan, let your taste buds be your guide on this delicious journey. Happy cooking!

Table of contents

Chapter 1

Sunrise Delights

2
burritos

350
calories

20 mins

Vegan Breakfast Burrito

Rise and shine with this plant-powered wonder!

Ingredients:

- 4 large tortillas
- 1 cup tofu scramble
- 1 cup black bean
- 1/2 cup diced tomatoes
- 1/2 cup diced bell peppers
- 1/4 cup diced red onion
- 1/4 cup vegan cheese
- 1/4 cup salsa - Salt and pepper to taste

Directions

1. Prepare the tofu scramble by sautéing crumbled tofu with spices until lightly browned.
2. Warm tortillas and assemble by adding tofu scramble, black beans, veggies, cheese, and salsa.
3. Roll them up, tuck in the sides, and enjoy!

Substitutions

None

2 servings

220 calories

15 mins

Tofu Scramble with Spinach and Mushrooms

A scramble that will make your taste buds dance!

Ingredients:

- 1/2 block of firm tofu, crumbled
- 1 cup spinach
- 1/2 cup mushrooms, sliced
- 1/4 cup diced onion
- 2 cloves garlic, minced
- 1 tbsp nutritional yeast
- Salt and pepper to taste

Directions

1. Sauté onions and garlic until fragrant.
2. Add mushrooms and cook until tender.
3. Stir in crumbled tofu and nutritional yeast, cook until heated through.
4. Add spinach, cook until wilted.
5. Season with salt and pepper.
6. Serve hot!

Substitutions

None

2 pancakes

180 calories

25 mins

Chickpea Pancakes with Avocado Salsa

A savory twist on pancakes to kickstart your day!

Ingredients:

- 1 cup chickpea flour
- 1/2 tsp baking powder
- 1/2 tsp cumin
- 1/2 tsp paprika
- Salt and pepper to taste
- 3/4 cup water
- 1 avocado, diced
- 1/2 cup cherry tomatoes, halved
- 2 tbsp chopped cilantro - Juice of 1 lime

Directions

1. Mix chickpea flour, baking powder, spices, and water to make batter.
2. Cook pancakes on a hot skillet until golden brown.
3. Mix avocado, tomatoes, cilantro, and lime juice for salsa.
4. Top pancakes with salsa and enjoy!

Substitutions

None

4
servings

280
calories

30 mins

Vegan Breakfast Hash

A hash that's a true morning masterpiece!

Ingredients:

- 4 cups diced potatoes
- 1 cup diced bell peppers
- 1/2 cup diced onion
- 1 cup black beans
- 1 cup spinach
- 2 cloves garlic, minced
- 1 tsp paprika
- Salt and pepper to taste

Directions

1. In a skillet, cook potatoes until crispy.
2. Add onions, peppers, and garlic; sauté until tender.
3. Stir in black beans, spinach, and spices; cook until spinach wilts.
4. Season with salt and pepper.
5. Serve hot!

Substitutions

None

2 quesadillas | 320 calories | 20 mins

Breakfast Quesadilla

A cheesy, gooey delight to start your day right!

Ingredients:

- 4 large tortillas
- 1 cup vegan cheese
- 1 cup tofu scramble
- 1/2 cup black beans
- 1/2 cup diced tomatoes
- 1/4 cup diced red onion
- 1/4 cup salsa
- Salt and pepper to taste

Directions

1. Place tortilla on a skillet, sprinkle with cheese.
2. Add tofu scramble, beans, veggies, and salsa.
3. Top with another tortilla, press gently.
4. Cook until golden, flip, and cook the other side.
5. Slice and enjoy!

Substitutions

None

4
servings

380
calories

35 mins

Vegan Biscuits and Gravy

A hearty Southern classic gone vegan!

Ingredients:

- 8 vegan biscuits
- 2 cups vegan sausage gravy (store-bought or homemade)
- Chopped fresh parsley for garnish (optional)

Directions

1. Bake biscuits as per package instructions.
2. Heat the vegan sausage gravy.
3. Pour gravy over split biscuits.
4. Garnish with parsley if desired.
5. Dive into comfort!

Substitutions

None

4 tacos

250 calories

15 mins

Easy

Vegan Breakfast Tacos

Tacos for breakfast? Absolutely!

Ingredients:

- 4 small tortillas
- 1 cup tofu scramble
- 1/2 cup black beans
- 1/2 cup diced tomatoes
- 1/4 cup diced red onion
- 1/4 cup salsa\n- Salt and pepper to taste

Directions

1. Warm tortillas and assemble with tofu scramble, beans, veggies, and salsa.
2. Season with salt and pepper.
3. Roll up and enjoy your morning fiesta!

Substitutions

None

2 sandwiches | 290 calories | 10 mins

Vegan Breakfast Sandwich

A handheld breakfast that's as satisfying as it is quick!

Ingredients:

- 4 slices whole-grain bread
- 1/2 cup avocado mash
- 1 cup baby spinach
- 1/2 cup sliced tomatoes
- Salt and pepper to taste

Directions

1. Spread avocado mash on bread slices.
2. Layer with spinach, tomatoes, and season with salt and pepper.
3. Top with another slice of bread.
4. Slice in half and devour!

Substitutions

None

2 pancakes

200 calories

30 mins

Blueberry Pancakes

Fluffy pancakes with a burst of blueberry goodness!

Ingredients:

- 1 cup all-purpose flour
- 1 tbsp sugar
- 1 tsp baking powder
- 1/2 tsp baking soda
- 1/2 tsp salt
- 1 cup almond milk
- 1 tbsp apple cider vinegar
- 1 tsp vanilla extract
- 1/2 cup blueberries

Directions

1. Mix dry ingredients in one bowl, wet ingredients in another.
2. Combine, then fold in blueberries.
3. Cook on a hot griddle until golden brown.
4. Serve with maple syrup!

Substitutions

None

1 bowl

350
calories

10 mins

Vegan Breakfast Bowl

A bowl of morning delight to fuel your day!

Ingredients:

- 1 cup cooked quinoa
- 1/2 cup mixed berries
- 1/4 cup chopped nuts
- 1 tbsp maple syrup
- 1/2 tsp cinnamon

Directions

1. Layer quinoa, berries, and nuts in a bowl.
2. Drizzle with maple syrup.
3. Sprinkle with cinnamon.
4. Dive in and enjoy!

Substitutions

None

Chapter 2

Midday Munchies

2 sandwiches

320 calories

25 mins

Vegan BBQ Pulled Jackfruit Sandwich

A smoky, sweet, and savory masterpiece between buns!

Ingredients:

- 1 can young jackfruit, drained and shredded
- 1/2 cup barbecue sauce
- 1/2 tsp smoked paprika
- 1/2 tsp garlic powder
- Salt and pepper to taste
- 4 whole-grain buns
- Coleslaw (optional)

Directions

1. In a pan, sauté shredded jackfruit until slightly crispy.
2. Add barbecue sauce, paprika, garlic powder, salt, and pepper.
3. Cook until jackfruit is coated and tender.
4. Serve on buns with coleslaw if desired.
5. Devour!

Substitutions

None

2 servings | 150 calories | 20 mins

Vegan Buffalo Cauliflower Bites

These bites are the definition of spicy satisfaction!

Ingredients:

- 1/2 head cauliflower, cut into florets
- 1/2 cup flour
- 1/2 cup water
- 1/2 tsp garlic powder
- 1/2 tsp onion powder
- 1/2 cup buffalo sauce
- Vegan ranch or blue cheese dressing (for dipping)

Directions

1. Preheat oven to 450°F (230°C).
2. In a bowl, mix flour, water, and spices to create a batter.
3. Dip cauliflower florets into the batter, letting excess drip off.
4. Place on a baking sheet and bake until crispy, about 15 mins.
5. Toss in buffalo sauce.
6. Serve with vegan ranch or blue cheese dressing.
7. Enjoy the heat!

Substitutions

None

2 wraps

280 calories

15 mins

Chickpea Salad Wrap

A satisfying wrap packed with protein and flavor!

Ingredients:

- 1 can chickpeas, drained and mashed
- 1/4 cup diced cucumber
- 1/4 cup diced bell pepper
- 1/4 cup diced red onion
- 1/4 cup chopped fresh parsley
- 2 tbsp lemon juice
- 2 tbsp tahini
- Salt and pepper to taste
- 2 whole-grain wraps

Directions

1. In a bowl, mix mashed chickpeas, veggies, parsley, lemon juice, tahini, salt, and pepper.
2. Divide the mixture between wraps.
3. Roll them up, and you're ready to go!
4. Savor every bite!

Substitutions

None

2 sandwiches | 260 calories | 15 mins

Vegan BLT Sandwich

A classic with a vegan twist that'll leave you craving more!

Ingredients:

- 4 slices whole-grain bread
- 1 cup tempeh bacon
- 1 cup lettuce
- 1 cup sliced tomatoes
- Vegan mayo
- Salt and pepper to taste

Directions

1. Cook tempeh bacon until crispy.
2. Toast the bread slices.
3. Spread vegan mayo on the bread.
4. Assemble sandwiches with tempeh bacon, lettuce, and tomatoes.
5. Season with salt and pepper.
6. Dive into deliciousness!

Substitutions

None

2 servings

220 calories

30 mins

Sweet Potato Fries with Vegan Aioli

Crispy fries with a creamy dip that's simply irresistible!

Ingredients:

- 2 medium sweet potatoes, cut into fries
- 1 tbsp olive oil
- 1/2 tsp paprika
- Salt and pepper to taste
- 1/2 cup vegan aioli (store-bought or homemade)

Directions

1. Preheat oven to 425°F (220°C).
2. Toss sweet potato fries with olive oil, paprika, salt, and pepper.
3. Bake until crispy, about 25 mins.
4. Serve with vegan aioli for dipping.
5. Enjoy the perfect combo!

Substitutions

None

2 sandwic hes | 380 calories | 35 mins

Vegan Philly Cheesesteak

A hearty, cheesy sandwich that's completely plant-based!

Ingredients:

- 2 sub rolls
- 1 cup sliced seitan or portobello mushrooms
- 1/2 cup sliced bell peppers
- 1/2 cup sliced onions
- 1/2 cup vegan cheese sauce
- Salt and pepper to taste

Directions

1. In a pan, sauté seitan or mushrooms, peppers, and onions until tender.
2. Warm sub rolls.
3. Fill rolls with sautéed mixture.
4. Pour vegan cheese sauce on top.
5. Season with salt and pepper.
6. Devour the Philly goodness!

Substitutions

None

2 servings

320 calories

20 mins

Normal

Vegan Thai Peanut Noodles

Creamy peanut sauce meets tender noodles in this Thai delight!

Ingredients:

- 6 oz rice noodles
- 1/4 cup peanut butter
- 2 tbsp soy sauce
- 2 tbsp lime juice
- 1 tbsp maple syrup
- 1 clove garlic, minced
- 1/2 tsp red pepper flakes (adjust to taste)
- Chopped peanuts and cilantro for garnish

Directions

1. Cook rice noodles according to package instructions.
2. In a bowl, whisk peanut butter, soy sauce, lime juice, maple syrup, garlic, and red pepper flakes.
3. Toss cooked noodles with peanut sauce.
4. Garnish with chopped peanuts and cilantro.
5. Savor every bite!

Substitutions

None

4 servings

290 calories

25 mins

Vegan Sloppy Joes

These messy delights are a vegan twist on a classic favorite!

Ingredients:

- 1 cup lentils (cooked and drained)
- 1 cup diced bell peppers
- 1/2 cup diced onion
- 1 cup tomato sauce
- 2 tbsp tomato paste
- 2 tbsp maple syrup
- 1 tbsp soy sauce
- 1 tsp chili powder (adjust to taste)
- Salt and pepper to taste
- 4 whole-grain buns

Directions

1. In a pan, sauté peppers and onions until softened.
2. Add cooked lentils, tomato sauce, tomato paste, maple syrup, soy sauce, chili powder, salt, and pepper.
3. Cook until heated through.
4. Serve on buns and embrace the messiness!

Substitutions

None

2 wraps

250 calories

30 mins

Vegan Falafel Wrap

A wrap bursting with Mediterranean flavors and crispy falafel!

Ingredients:

- 4 whole-grain wraps
- 8 falafel patties (store-bought or homemade)
- 1 cup chopped lettuce
- 1/2 cup diced tomatoes
- 1/4 cup diced cucumber
- 1/4 cup diced red onion
- Vegan tahini sauce

Directions

1. Warm falafel patties according to package instructions.
2. Warm wraps.
3. Assemble wraps with falafel, lettuce, tomatoes, cucumber, red onion, and a drizzle of tahini sauce.
4. Roll them up and indulge in the Mediterranean goodness!

Substitutions

None

4 servings

290 calories

20 mins

Easy

Vegan Pesto Pasta Salad

A refreshing pasta salad kissed by the flavors of basil and pine nuts!

Ingredients:

- 8 oz pasta of your choice (cooked and cooled)
- 1/2 cup vegan pesto sauce
- 1 cup cherry tomatoes, halved
- 1/2 cup diced cucumber
- 1/4 cup pine nuts, toasted
- Fresh basil leaves for garnish

Directions

1. In a large bowl, combine cooked pasta, vegan pesto, cherry tomatoes, cucumber, and toasted pine nuts.
2. Toss until well coated.
3. Garnish with fresh basil leaves.
4. Serve chilled and enjoy the summery goodness!

Substitutions

None

Chapter 3
Dinner Delights

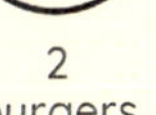

2
burgers

280
calories

30 mins

Vegan Black Bean Burger

A burger that's hearty, flavorful, and completely plant-based!

Ingredients:

- 1 can black beans, drained and rinsed
- 1/2 cup breadcrumbs
- 1/4 cup diced onion
- 1/4 cup diced bell pepper
- 2 cloves garlic, minced
- 1 tsp cumin
- 1 tsp chili powder
- Salt and pepper to taste
- 2 whole-grain burger buns
- Lettuce, tomato, and your favorite burger toppings

Directions

1. Mash black beans in a bowl, leaving some chunks for texture.
2. Mix in breadcrumbs, onion, bell pepper, garlic, and spices.
3. Form into burger patties.
4. Grill or cook in a pan until browned and heated through.
5. Assemble with your favorite toppings on buns.
6. Bite into burger bliss!

Substitutions

None

2 servings

230 calories

25 mins

Vegan Tofu Stir-Fry

A stir-fry bursting with colorful veggies and tofu goodness!

Ingredients:

- 8 oz tofu, cubed
- 2 cups mixed vegetables (bell peppers, broccoli, carrots, snap peas, etc.)
- 2 cloves garlic, minced
- 2 tbsp soy sauce
- 1 tbsp sesame oil
- 1 tbsp maple syrup
- 1/2 tsp ginger, minced
- Cooked rice or noodles for serving

Directions

1. In a pan, sauté tofu until lightly browned, then set aside.
2. In the same pan, sauté garlic and veggies until tender.
3. Mix in soy sauce, sesame oil, maple syrup, and ginger.
4. Add tofu back in, heat through.
5. Serve over cooked rice or noodles.
6. Enjoy the tofu-tastic stir-fry!

Substitutions

None

4 servings | 300 calories | 40 mins

Vegan Chili

A warm and comforting chili that's perfect for chilly evenings!

Ingredients:

- 1 can kidney beans, drained and rinsed
- 1 can black beans, drained and rinsed
- 1 can diced tomatoes
- 1 cup vegetable broth
- 1 cup diced bell peppers
- 1 cup diced onion
- 1 cup corn kernels
- 2 cloves garlic, minced
- 2 tbsp chili powder
- 1 tsp cumin
- Salt and pepper to taste

Directions

1. In a pot, sauté onion and garlic until fragrant.
2. Add bell peppers and cook until tender.
3. Stir in beans, diced tomatoes, vegetable broth, corn, and spices.
4. Simmer for 30 minutes, stirring occasionally.
5. Season with salt and pepper.
6. Ladle into bowls and savor the warmth!

Substitutions

None

4 servings

350 calories

25 mins

Vegan Mac and Cheese

Creamy and cheesy macaroni that's dairy-free and delightful!

Ingredients:

- 8 oz macaroni or pasta of your choice (cooked)
- 1 cup raw cashews, soaked and drained
- 1 cup water
- 1/4 cup nutritional yeast
- 1/4 cup diced carrots
- 1/4 cup diced onion
- 1/4 cup diced potatoes
- 2 cloves garlic, minced
- 1/2 tsp turmeric (for color)
- Salt and pepper to taste

Directions

1. In a blender, combine soaked cashews, water, nutritional yeast, carrots, onion, potatoes, garlic, turmeric, salt, and pepper.
2. Blend until smooth and creamy.
3. Toss cooked pasta with the sauce.
4. Warm if needed, and serve.
5. Dive into creamy mac and cheese heaven!

Substitutions

None

4 servings

320 calories

35 mins

Vegan Spaghetti Bolognese

A vegan twist on a classic Italian favorite!

Ingredients:

- 8 oz spaghetti
 1 cup TVP (Textured Vegetable Protein), rehydrated
- 1 can crushed tomatoes
- 1 cup diced onion
- 1/2 cup diced carrots
- 1/2 cup diced celery
- 2 cloves garlic, minced
- 2 tbsp tomato paste
- 1 tsp dried basil
- 1 tsp dried oregano
- Salt and pepper to taste

Directions

1. Cook spaghetti according to package instructions.
2. In a pan, sauté onion, carrots, celery, and garlic until tender.
3. Stir in rehydrated TVP, crushed tomatoes, tomato paste, basil, oregano, salt, and pepper.
4. Simmer for 20 minutes.
5. Serve over cooked spaghetti.
6. Enjoy the Italian flavors!

Substitutions

None

4 rolls

250 calories

40 mins

Vegan Sushi Rolls

Roll your own sushi with a delightful vegan twist!

Ingredients:

- 1 cup sushi rice, cooked and seasoned with rice vinegar and sugar
- 4 nori seaweed sheets
- Assorted veggies (avocado, cucumber, bell pepper, carrot, etc.)
- Baked or marinated tofu strips
- Soy sauce and wasabi (for dipping)

Directions

1. Place a bamboo sushi rolling mat on a clean surface.
2. Lay a sheet of plastic wrap on the mat.
3. Place a nori sheet on the plastic wrap.
4. Spread a thin layer of sushi rice on the nori, leaving a border.
5. Add veggies and tofu strips.
6. Roll it up tightly, using the mat to help.
7. Slice into bite-sized pieces.
8. Serve with soy sauce and wasabi.
9. Enjoy your homemade sushi!

Substitutions

None

4
servings

280
calories

30 mins

Vegan Pad Thai

A tangy and satisfying noodle dish with Thai flavors!

Ingredients:

- 8 oz rice noodles, cooked and drained
- 1 cup tofu, cubed
- 1 cup mixed vegetables (bean sprouts, bell peppers, green onions, etc.)
- 2 cloves garlic, minced
- 2 tbsp soy sauce
- 2 tbsp tamarind paste
- 1 tbsp maple syrup
- 1/2 tsp red pepper flakes (adjust to taste)
- Crushed peanuts and lime wedges for garnish

Directions

1. In a pan, sauté tofu until lightly browned, then set aside.
2. In the same pan, sauté garlic and mixed veggies until tender.
3. Add cooked noodles, soy sauce, tamarind paste, maple syrup, and red pepper flakes.
4. Stir-fry until heated through.
5. Garnish with crushed peanuts and lime wedges.
6. Enjoy the Pad Thai goodness!

Substitutions

None

4
enchiladas

320
calories

35 mins

Vegan Enchiladas

A saucy, spicy, and satisfying Mexican fiesta on a plate!

Ingredients:

- 4 whole-grain tortillas
- 1 cup cooked black beans
- 1 cup cooked quinoa
- 1 cup diced bell peppers
- 1 cup corn kernels
- 1 cup enchilada sauce (store-bought or homemade)
- 1/2 cup diced onion
- 1/2 cup diced tomatoes
- 1/4 cup vegan cheese (optional)
- Chopped cilantro for garnish

Directions

1. Preheat oven to 375°F (190°C).
2. Mix black beans, quinoa, bell peppers, and corn in a bowl.
3. Fill tortillas with the mixture, roll up, and place in a baking dish.
4. Pour enchilada sauce over the top.
5. Sprinkle with diced onion, tomatoes, and vegan cheese if desired.
6. Bake for 20 minutes until bubbly.
7. Garnish with cilantro.
8. Dive into enchilada heaven!

Substitutions

None

Vegan Mushroom Stroganoff

A creamy and rich mushroom stroganoff without the dairy!

Ingredients:

- 8 oz pasta of your choice (cooked)
- 2 cups sliced mushrooms
- 1 cup diced onion
- 2 cloves garlic, minced
- 1/2 cup vegetable broth
- 1 cup cashew cream (blend soaked cashews with water until smooth)
- 1 tbsp soy sauce
- 1 tsp Dijon mustard
- 1 tsp paprika
- Salt and pepper to taste

Directions

1. In a pan, sauté mushrooms until browned, then set aside.
2. In the same pan, sauté onion and garlic until tender.
3. Add vegetable broth, cashew cream, soy sauce, Dijon mustard, paprika, salt, and pepper.
4. Stir until it thickens.
5. Add sautéed mushrooms.
6. Serve over cooked pasta.
7. Enjoy the creamy stroganoff!

Substitutions

None

2 servings

350 calories

40 mins

Hard

Vegan BBQ Ribs

Sticky, smoky, and utterly satisfying vegan BBQ ribs!

Ingredients:

- 1 cup vital wheat gluten
- 2 tbsp nutritional yeast
- 1 tsp smoked paprika
- 1/2 tsp garlic powder
- 1/2 tsp onion powder
- 1/2 cup vegetable broth
- 1/4 cup barbecue sauce
- 2 tbsp soy sauce
- 1 tbsp olive oil
- 1 tbsp tomato paste
- Salt and pepper to taste

Directions

1. In a bowl, mix vital wheat gluten, nutritional yeast, smoked paprika, garlic powder, and onion powder.
2. In another bowl, whisk together vegetable broth, barbecue sauce, soy sauce, olive oil, tomato paste, salt, and pepper.
3. Pour wet mixture into dry mixture and knead to form a dough.
4. Shape into rib-like pieces.
5. Steam ribs for 30 minutes.
6. Grill or bake, brushing with barbecue sauce until caramelized.
7. Savor the BBQ rib goodness!

Substitutions

None

Chapter 4
International Flavors

4 servings

320 calories

35 mins

Vegan Tikka Masala

A creamy and flavorful Indian favorite gone vegan!

Ingredients:

- 1 cup tofu cubes
- 1 cup diced bell peppers
- 1 cup diced onion
- 2 cloves garlic, minced
- 1 tbsp ginger, minced
- 1 can chickpeas, drained and rinsed
- 1 can diced tomatoes
- 1/2 cup canned coconut milk
- 2 tbsp tomato paste
- 2 tbsp garam masala
- 1 tsp turmeric
- 1/2 tsp chili powder (adjust to taste)
- Salt and pepper to taste
- Fresh cilantro for garnish
- Cooked rice for serving

Substitutions

None

Directions

1. In a pan, sauté tofu until lightly browned, then set aside.
2. In the same pan, sauté onion, garlic, and ginger until fragrant.
3. Add bell peppers, chickpeas, diced tomatoes, coconut milk, tomato paste, and spices.
4. Simmer for 15 minutes.
5. Season with salt and pepper.
6. Add tofu back in, heat through.
7. Serve over cooked rice, garnish with fresh cilantro.
8. Enjoy the Tikka Masala bliss!

4
servings

280
calories

30 mins

Normal

Vegan Shawarma

A Middle Eastern delight filled with spiced goodness!

Ingredients:

- 8 oz seitan or tempeh, sliced
- 4 whole-grain pitas or flatbreads
- 1 cup sliced cucumber
- 1 cup sliced tomatoes
- 1/2 cup sliced red onion
- 1/4 cup chopped fresh parsley
- Vegan tahini sauce or yogurt sauce
- 1 tsp ground cumin
- 1 tsp paprika
- 1/2 tsp ground cinnamon
- Salt and pepper to taste

Directions

1. In a pan, sauté seitan or tempeh until lightly browned, then add spices and heat through.
2. Warm pitas or flatbreads.
3. Assemble sandwiches with seitan or tempeh, cucumber, tomatoes, red onion, parsley, and a drizzle of tahini or yogurt sauce.
4. Sprinkle with more spices if desired.
5. Roll up and savor the shawarma goodness!

Substitutions

None

4 tacos | 260 calories | 35 mins

Vegan Tacos al Pastor

Tacos with a Mexican twist, full of smoky flavors!

Ingredients:

- 2 cups cooked short-grain rice
- 1 cup sliced tofu or tempeh, sautéed
- 1 cup mixed vegetables (spinach, carrots, zucchini, bean sprouts, etc.), blanched and seasoned
- 1/4 cup kimchi
- 4 fried or poached vegan eggs (optional)
- 4 tbsp gochujang sauce (adjust to taste)
- Sesame oil and sesame seeds for garnish

Directions

1. In a pan, sauté shredded jackfruit, garlic, chili powder, cumin, smoked paprika, salt, and pepper until heated through.
2. Warm tortillas.
3. Assemble tacos with jackfruit, pineapple, red onion, cilantro, and a squeeze of lime.
4. Roll them up and enjoy the tacos al pastor!

Substitutions

None

4 servings

300 calories

40 mins

Vegan Korean Bibimbap

A Korean rice bowl that's a harmony of flavors and colors!

Ingredients:

- 2 cups cooked short-grain rice
- 1 cup sliced tofu or tempeh, sautéed
- 1 cup mixed vegetables (spinach, carrots, zucchini, bean sprouts, etc.), blanched and seasoned
- 1/4 cup kimchi
- 4 fried or poached vegan eggs (optional)
- 4 tbsp gochujang sauce (adjust to taste)
- Sesame oil and sesame seeds for garnish

Directions

1. Divide cooked rice into four bowls.
2. Arrange sautéed tofu or tempeh, blanched veggies, kimchi, and vegan eggs if using.
3. Drizzle with gochujang sauce and a splash of sesame oil.
4. Sprinkle with sesame seeds.
5. Mix before eating to combine all the flavors.
6. Enjoy the bibimbap medley!

Substitutions

None

4 servings | 350 calories | 40 mins

Vegan Thai Green Curry

A fragrant Thai curry brimming with vegetables and tofu!

Ingredients:

- 1 cup cubed tofu
- 1 cup sliced bell peppers
- 1 cup sliced zucchini
- 1 cup sliced carrots
- 1 cup broccoli florets
- 2 cups coconut milk
- 2 tbsp green curry paste (adjust to taste)
- 1 tbsp soy sauce
- 1 tbsp brown sugar
- Salt and pepper to taste
- Cooked rice for serving
- Fresh cilantro for garnish

Substitutions

None

Directions

1. In a pot, sauté tofu until lightly browned, then set aside.
2. In the same pot, add green curry paste and coconut milk, stir until combined.
3. Add vegetables, soy sauce, brown sugar, salt, and pepper.
4. Simmer for 20 minutes until veggies are tender.
5. Add tofu back in, heat through.
6. Serve over cooked rice, garnish with fresh cilantro.
7. Savor the Thai green curry!

4 gyros | 320 calories | 35 mins

Vegan Gyros

Greek-style sandwiches bursting with Mediterranean flavors!

Ingredients:

- 4 whole-grain pitas or flatbreads
- 1 cup sliced seitan or marinated mushrooms
- 1 cup sliced cucumber
- 1/2 cup diced tomatoes
- 1/4 cup sliced red onion
- Vegan tzatziki sauce
- 1 tsp dried oregano
- 1/2 tsp garlic powder
- Salt and pepper to taste

Directions

1. Warm pitas or flatbreads.
2. Sauté seitan or mushrooms until heated through, sprinkle with oregano, garlic powder, salt, and pepper.
3. Assemble sandwiches with seitan or mushrooms, cucumber, tomatoes, red onion, and a drizzle of tzatziki sauce.
4. Roll them up and savor the gyro flavors!

Substitutions

None

4 sandwiches | 290 calories | 30 mins

Vegan Cuban Sandwich

A Cuban delight filled with layers of flavor and textures!

Ingredients:

- 4 whole-grain rolls
- 1 cup sliced seitan or marinated mushrooms
- 1 cup sliced pickles
- 1/2 cup sliced vegan ham (optional)
- 1/2 cup vegan Swiss cheese slices (optional)
- Yellow mustard
- 1 tsp dried oregano
- Salt and pepper to taste

Directions

1. Slice rolls in half and spread yellow mustard on both sides.
2. Layer seitan or mushrooms, pickles, vegan ham, and vegan Swiss cheese if using.
3. Sprinkle with oregano, salt, and pepper.
4. Press sandwiches in a panini press or grill until crispy and cheese is melted.
5. Dive into the Cuban sandwich goodness!

Substitutions

None

4 servings | 340 calories | 40 mins

Vegan Moroccan Tagine

A Moroccan-inspired stew that's a symphony of spices and textures!

Ingredients:

- 1 cup diced tofu or tempeh
- 1 cup diced eggplant
- 1 cup diced zucchini
- 1 cup diced bell peppers
- 1 cup diced tomatoes
- 1/2 cup sliced dried apricots
- 1/4 cup sliced almonds, toasted
- 1 cup vegetable broth
- 2 tbsp Moroccan spice blend (adjust to taste)
- Olive oil
- Salt and pepper to taste

Substitutions

None

Directions

1. In a tagine or a large pan, sauté tofu or tempeh until lightly browned, then set aside.
2. In the same tagine or pan, add olive oil and sauté eggplant, zucchini, and bell peppers until tender.
3. Add diced tomatoes, apricots, and toasted almonds.
4. Sprinkle with Moroccan spice blend, salt, and pepper.
5. Add tofu or tempeh back in, stir to combine.
6. Pour in vegetable broth, cover, and simmer for 20 minutes.
7. Enjoy the Moroccan tagine!

4 servings

280 calories

30 mins

Vegan Vegetable Ramen

A comforting bowl of ramen with a vegan twist!

Ingredients:

- 8 oz ramen noodles
- 4 cups vegetable broth
- 1 cup sliced mushrooms
- 1 cup sliced bok choy or spinach
- 1 cup sliced carrots
- 1 cup sliced green onions
- 1/4 cup miso paste
- 1 tbsp soy sauce
- 1 tbsp sesame oil
- 1 tsp grated ginger
- 2 cloves garlic, minced
- Salt and pepper to taste

Directions

1. Cook ramen noodles according to package instructions.
2. In a pot, bring vegetable broth to a simmer.
3. Add mushrooms, bok choy or spinach, carrots, green onions, miso paste, soy sauce, sesame oil, ginger, garlic, salt, and pepper.
4. Simmer until veggies are tender.
5. Serve over cooked ramen noodles.
6. Enjoy the comforting vegetable ramen!

Substitutions

None

4
servings

180
calories

15 mins

Vegan Greek Salad

A refreshing and tangy Greek salad with a vegan twist!

Ingredients:

- 4 cups mixed greens
- 1 cup sliced cucumber
- 1 cup diced tomatoes
- 1/2 cup sliced Kalamata olives
- 1/4 cup sliced red onion
- 1/4 cup diced vegan feta cheese (store-bought or homemade)
- 2 tbsp extra-virgin olive oil
- 2 tbsp red wine vinegar
- 1 tsp dried oregano
- Salt and pepper to taste

Directions

1. In a large bowl, combine mixed greens, cucumber, tomatoes, Kalamata olives, red onion, and vegan feta cheese.
2. In a small bowl, whisk together olive oil, red wine vinegar, dried oregano, salt, and pepper.
3. Drizzle the dressing over the salad and toss to combine.
4. Serve and savor the Greek flavors!

Substitutions

None

We have a small favor to ask

Right in the midst of this culinary rollercoaster, as we navigate through the savory twists and tantalizing turns of the Fast Food Vegan Cookbook, I want to pause for a moment and talk about something crucial – reviews. These little nuggets of feedback are like the hidden gems in the culinary world. They can make or break a dining experience, or in this case, a cookbook.

You see, reviews are a rare and precious currency in the realm of books. They're as elusive as the perfect fusion of flavors in a complex sauce, and yet, they're the lifeblood of any author or small publisher. In this world where fast food reigns supreme, a few words from you can have a monumental impact.

So, here's my humble plea to you, dear reader. If these plant-based, fast-food-inspired recipes have tantalized your taste buds and brought a new dimension to your vegan journey, would you consider taking a moment? Head back to your app or wherever you procured this culinary adventure, and you'll discover that magical review button. Give us a star rating and share a brief sentence or two about your experience. It's like adding the perfect garnish to a dish, enhancing the overall flavor.

Being a small publisher, every review is a beacon of light guiding us through the foggy maze of the publishing world. Your words can inspire more people to explore the joys of fast food made vegan, to savor the familiar tastes in a plant-based twist.

Rest assured, every review is not just valued but cherished. We understand that, just like in the heat of a busy kitchen, even the most seasoned chefs can make a minor misstep. If you happen to spot any such hiccup along your culinary journey within these pages, please know that we've poured our hearts and souls into this cookbook. We're human, and in the art of cooking, a small mistake now and then is part of the creative process.

Now, let's get back to what we love most – the recipes. As we journey through these pages, may you continue to explore, savor, and enjoy the delicious world of fast food made vegan. Thank you for considering leaving a review, and thank you for being part of this delectable adventure.

Chapter 5
Hearty Bowls

4
servings

300
calories

30 mins

Vegan Buddha Bowl

A wholesome and balanced bowl that's a feast for the senses!

Ingredients:

- 2 cups cooked quinoa
- 1 cup roasted chickpeas
- 2 cups mixed greens
- 1 cup roasted sweet potatoes
- 1 cup sliced cucumber
- 1/2 cup shredded carrots
- 1/4 cup hummus
- 1/4 cup tahini sauce
- 1/4 cup chopped fresh cilantro
- Lemon wedges for garnish

Directions

1. Divide cooked quinoa into four bowls.
2. Arrange roasted chickpeas, mixed greens, roasted sweet potatoes, cucumber, and shredded carrots on top.
3. Drizzle with hummus and tahini sauce.
4. Sprinkle with fresh cilantro.
5. Serve with lemon wedges for an extra zing.
6. Savor the Buddha bowl goodness!

Substitutions

None

4 servings

320 calories

35 mins

Vegan Burrito Bowl

All the flavors of a burrito, deconstructed into a bowl!

Ingredients:

- 2 cups cooked brown rice
- 1 cup black beans, drained and rinsed
- 1 cup corn kernels (fresh or frozen)
- 1 cup diced tomatoes
- 1/2 cup diced red onion
- 1/2 cup diced bell peppers
- 1/4 cup chopped fresh cilantro
- 1/4 cup diced avocado
- 1/4 cup vegan sour cream
- 1/4 cup salsa
- 1 tsp chili powder
- 1/2 tsp ground cumin
- Salt and pepper to taste

Directions

1. Divide cooked brown rice into four bowls.
2. Top with black beans, corn kernels, diced tomatoes, red onion, bell peppers, and chopped cilantro.
3. Drizzle with vegan sour cream and salsa.
4. Sprinkle with diced avocado.
5. Season with chili powder, ground cumin, salt, and pepper.
6. Enjoy the burrito bowl fiesta!

Substitutions

None

4 servings | 280 calories | 25 mins

Vegan Quinoa Salad

A light and refreshing salad with protein-packed quinoa!

Ingredients:

- 2 cups cooked quinoa
- 1 cup diced cucumber
- 1 cup diced tomatoes
- 1/2 cup diced red onion
- 1/2 cup diced bell peppers (assorted colors)
- 1/4 cup chopped fresh parsley
- 1/4 cup chopped fresh mint
- Juice of 2 lemons
- 2 tbsp extra-virgin olive oil
- Salt and pepper to taste

Directions

1. In a large bowl, combine cooked quinoa, cucumber, tomatoes, red onion, bell peppers, parsley, and mint.
2. In a small bowl, whisk together lemon juice, olive oil, salt, and pepper.
3. Drizzle the dressing over the salad and toss to combine.
4. Serve and savor the quinoa salad freshness!

Substitutions

None

4
servings

320
calories

30 mins

Vegan Teriyaki Bowl

A savory and sweet bowl with vegan teriyaki goodness!

Ingredients:

- 2 cups cooked brown rice
- 1 cup sliced tofu, sautéed or baked
- 1 cup steamed broccoli florets
- 1 cup sliced bell peppers (assorted colors)
- 1/2 cup sliced carrots
- 1/4 cup sliced green onions
- 1/4 cup teriyaki sauce (store-bought or homemade)
- Sesame seeds for garnish

Directions

1. Divide cooked brown rice into four bowls.
2. Arrange sautéed or baked tofu, steamed broccoli, bell peppers, carrots, and green onions on top.
3. Drizzle with teriyaki sauce.
4. Sprinkle with sesame seeds.
5. Enjoy the teriyaki bowl goodness!

Substitutions

None

4 servings | 280 calories | 25 mins

Easy

Vegan Taco Salad

A salad that's a fiesta of flavors, inspired by tacos!

Ingredients:

- 4 cups mixed greens
- 1 cup cooked black beans, drained and rinsed
- 1 cup cooked corn kernels (fresh or frozen)
- 1 cup diced tomatoes
- 1/2 cup diced red onion
- 1/2 cup diced avocado
- 1/4 cup chopped fresh cilantro
- 1/4 cup crushed tortilla chips
- 1/4 cup salsa
- 1/4 cup vegan sour cream
- 1 tsp chili powder
- 1/2 tsp ground cumin
- Salt and pepper to taste

Directions

1. Divide mixed greens into four bowls.
2. Top with black beans, corn kernels, diced tomatoes, red onion, avocado, and chopped cilantro.
3. Sprinkle with crushed tortilla chips.
4. Drizzle with salsa and vegan sour cream.
5. Season with chili powder, ground cumin, salt, and pepper.
6. Enjoy the taco salad fiesta!

Substitutions

None

4
servings

350
calories

40 mins

Vegan Grain Bowl with Tahini Dressing

A satisfying grain bowl with creamy tahini dressing!

Ingredients:

- 2 cups cooked grains (quinoa, farro, or your choice)
- 1 cup roasted chickpeas
- 1 cup roasted sweet potatoes
- 1 cup steamed broccoli
- 1 cup sliced cucumber
- 1/2 cup shredded carrots
- 1/4 cup chopped fresh parsley
- 1/4 cup chopped fresh mint
- 1/4 cup tahini dressing (tahini, lemon juice, garlic, water, salt)
- Lemon wedges for garnish

Directions

1. Divide cooked grains into four bowls.
2. Arrange roasted chickpeas, roasted sweet potatoes, steamed broccoli, cucumber, and shredded carrots on top.
3. Drizzle with tahini dressing.
4. Sprinkle with fresh parsley.
5. Serve with lemon wedges for an extra zing.
6. Savor the grain bowl with tahini goodness!

Substitutions

None

4 servings

290 calories

35 mins

Easy

Vegan Soba Noodle Bowl

A noodle bowl with the goodness of soba and veggies!

Ingredients:

- 8 oz soba noodles, cooked and drained
- 1 cup sliced tofu, sautéed or baked
- 1 cup sliced bell peppers (assorted colors)
- 1 cup sliced cucumber
- 1/2 cup shredded carrots
- 1/4 cup chopped fresh cilantro
- 1/4 cup chopped green onions
- 1/4 cup sesame ginger dressing (store-bought or homemade)
- Sesame seeds for garnish

Directions

1. Divide cooked soba noodles into four bowls.
2. Arrange sautéed or baked tofu, bell peppers, cucumber, shredded carrots, cilantro, and green onions on top.
3. Drizzle with sesame ginger dressing.
4. Sprinkle with sesame seeds.
5. Enjoy the soba noodle bowl goodness!

Substitutions

None

4 servings

330 calories

35 mins

Easy

Vegan Power Bowl with Chickpeas

A power-packed bowl with protein-rich chickpeas!

Ingredients:

- 2 cups cooked quinoa
- 1 cup roasted chickpeas
- 1 cup steamed broccoli
- 1 cup sliced bell peppers (assorted colors)
- 1/2 cup shredded carrots
- 1/4 cup sliced Kalamata olives
- 1/4 cup tahini dressing (tahini, lemon juice, garlic, water, salt)
- Lemon wedges for garnish

Directions

1. Divide cooked quinoa into four bowls.
2. Arrange roasted chickpeas, steamed broccoli, bell peppers, shredded carrots, Kalamata olives, and tahini dressing on top.
3. Serve with lemon wedges for an extra zing.
4. Savor the power bowl with chickpeas!

Substitutions

None

4 servings

340 calories

40 mins

Easy

Vegan Bibimbap Bowl

A Korean rice bowl with a colorful array of toppings!

Ingredients:

- 2 cups cooked short-grain rice
- 1 cup sliced tofu or tempeh, sautéed
- 1 cup mixed vegetables (spinach, carrots, zucchini, bean sprouts, etc.), blanched and seasoned
- 1/4 cup kimchi
- 4 fried or poached vegan eggs (optional)
- 4 tbsp gochujang sauce (adjust to taste)
- Sesame oil and sesame seeds for garnish

Directions

1. Divide cooked rice into four bowls.
2. Arrange sautéed tofu or tempeh, blanched veggies, kimchi, and vegan eggs if using.
3. Drizzle with gochujang sauce and a splash of sesame oil.
4. Sprinkle with sesame seeds.
5. Mix before eating to combine all the flavors.
6. Enjoy the Bibimbap medley!

Substitutions

None

4 servings

270 calories

30 mins

Vegan Mediterranean Bowl

A Mediterranean-inspired bowl with fresh and savory flavors!

Ingredients:

- 2 cups cooked quinoa
- 1 cup sliced cucumber
- 1 cup diced tomatoes
- 1/2 cup sliced Kalamata olives
- 1/4 cup diced red onion
- 1/4 cup diced vegan feta cheese (store-bought or homemade)
- 2 tbsp extra-virgin olive oil
- 2 tbsp red wine vinegar
- 1 tsp dried oregano
- Salt and pepper to taste

Directions

1. Divide cooked quinoa into four bowls.
2. Top with cucumber, tomatoes, Kalamata olives, red onion, and vegan feta cheese.
3. In a small bowl, whisk together olive oil, red wine vinegar, dried oregano, salt, and pepper.
4. Drizzle the dressing over the bowl.
5. Savor the Mediterranean bowl goodness!

Substitutions

None

Chapter 6
Comfort Classics

4 servings

280 calories

40 mins

Vegan Shepherd's Pie

A hearty and comforting classic with a vegan twist!

Ingredients:

- 2 cups mashed potatoes
- 1 cup cooked lentils
- 1 cup mixed vegetables (peas, carrots, corn)
- 1/2 cup diced onion
- 1/2 cup vegetable broth
- 2 cloves garlic, minced
- 2 tbsp tomato paste
- 1 tbsp soy sauce
- 1 tsp dried thyme
- Salt and pepper to taste

Directions

1. In a pan, sauté diced onion and garlic until tender.
2. Add cooked lentils, mixed vegetables, vegetable broth, tomato paste, soy sauce, dried thyme, salt, and pepper.
3. Simmer for 10 minutes until heated through.
4. Preheat oven to 375°F (190°C).
5. Spread the lentil and vegetable mixture in a baking dish.
6. Top with mashed potatoes.
7. Bake for 20 minutes until the top is golden.
8. Enjoy the Shepherd's Pie comfort!

Substitutions

None

4 servings | 320 calories | 45 mins

Vegan Lasagna

Layers of pasta, rich sauce, and creamy vegan goodness!

Ingredients:

- 8 lasagna noodles, cooked and drained
- 2 cups vegan ricotta cheese
- 2 cups vegan mozzarella cheese
- 2 cups vegan marinara sauce (store-bought or homemade)
- 1 cup chopped spinach
- 1/2 cup diced onion
- 2 cloves garlic, minced
- 1 tsp dried basil
- 1 tsp dried oregano
- Salt and pepper to taste

Substitutions

None

Directions

1. Preheat oven to 375°F (190°C).
2. In a pan, sauté diced onion and garlic until tender.
3. Stir in chopped spinach, dried basil, dried oregano, salt, and pepper.
4. In a baking dish, layer marinara sauce, lasagna noodles, vegan ricotta cheese, and the spinach mixture.
5. Repeat the layers, finishing with a layer of marinara sauce on top.
6. Sprinkle vegan mozzarella cheese over the final layer.
7. Bake for 25-30 minutes until bubbly and golden.
8. Enjoy the comforting Vegan Lasagna!

4 servings

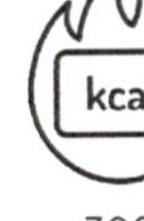

380 calories

45 mins

Vegan Chicken and Waffles

A classic brunch favorite, made vegan and delicious!

Ingredients:

- 2 cups vegan waffle batter (store-bought or homemade)
- 1 cup vegan chicken tenders (store-bought or homemade)
- 1/4 cup maple syrup
- Vegan butter for waffles
- Cooking oil for frying
- Salt and pepper to taste

Directions

1. Preheat a waffle iron and cook waffles according to the instructions, adding vegan butter to prevent sticking.
2. In a pan, heat cooking oil and fry vegan chicken tenders until golden and crispy.
3. Serve waffles with vegan chicken tenders.
4. Drizzle with maple syrup.
5. Season with salt and pepper if desired.
6. Enjoy the vegan Chicken and Waffles brunch!

Substitutions

None

4 servings

320 calories

45 mins

Vegan Meatloaf

A savory and hearty meatloaf that's entirely plant-based!

Ingredients:

- 2 cups cooked lentils
- 1 cup rolled oats
- 1/2 cup diced onion
- 1/2 cup diced bell peppers
- 1/4 cup tomato sauce
- 2 cloves garlic, minced
- 2 tbsp soy sauce
- 1 tbsp vegan Worcestershire sauce
- 1 tsp dried thyme
- Salt and pepper to taste

Directions

1. Preheat oven to 375°F (190°C).
2. In a food processor, combine cooked lentils, rolled oats, diced onion, diced bell peppers, tomato sauce, minced garlic, soy sauce, vegan Worcestershire sauce, dried thyme, salt, and pepper.
3. Pulse until the mixture is combined but still slightly chunky.
4. Transfer the mixture to a loaf pan and press it down.
5. Bake for 25-30 minutes until firm and slightly crispy on top.
6. Enjoy the hearty Vegan Meatloaf!

Substitutions

None

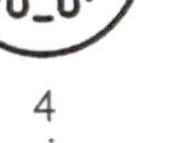

4 servings

290 calories

50 mins

Vegan Stuffed Bell Peppers

Bell peppers filled with a flavorful vegan stuffing!

Ingredients:

- 4 bell peppers, tops and seeds removed
- 1 cup cooked quinoa
- 1 cup diced tomatoes
- 1 cup black beans, drained and rinsed
- 1/2 cup diced onion
- 1/2 cup corn kernels (fresh or frozen)
- 1/4 cup vegan cheese shreds (optional)
- 2 cloves garlic, minced
- 1 tsp chili powder
- 1/2 tsp ground cumin
- Salt and pepper to taste

Directions

1. Preheat oven to 375°F (190°C).
2. In a bowl, combine cooked quinoa, diced tomatoes, black beans, diced onion, corn kernels, vegan cheese shreds if using, minced garlic, chili powder, ground cumin, salt, and pepper.
3. Stuff the mixture into the hollowed bell peppers.
4. Place stuffed peppers in a baking dish.
5. Cover with foil and bake for 30 minutes.
6. Remove foil and bake for an additional 10-15 minutes until peppers are tender.
7. Enjoy the Vegan Stuffed Bell Peppers!

Substitutions

None

4 servings | 340 calories | 45 mins

Vegan Baked Ziti

Ziti pasta smothered in a rich and creamy vegan sauce!

Ingredients:

- 8 oz ziti pasta, cooked and drained
- 2 cups vegan marinara sauce (store-bought or homemade)
- 1 cup vegan ricotta cheese
- 1 cup vegan mozzarella cheese
- 1/2 cup chopped spinach
- 1/2 cup diced onion
- 2 cloves garlic, minced
- 1 tsp dried basil
- 1 tsp dried oregano
- Salt and pepper to taste

Substitutions

None

Directions

1. Preheat oven to 375°F (190°C).
2. In a pan, sauté diced onion and garlic until tender.
3. Stir in chopped spinach, dried basil, dried oregano, salt, and pepper.
4. In a baking dish, layer cooked ziti pasta, marinara sauce, vegan ricotta cheese, and the spinach mixture.
5. Repeat the layers, finishing with a layer of marinara sauce on top.
6. Sprinkle vegan mozzarella cheese over the final layer.
7. Bake for 25-30 minutes until bubbly and golden.
8. Enjoy the comforting Vegan Baked Ziti!

4 servings | 320 calories | 50 mins

Vegan Pot Pie

A flaky and comforting pot pie filled with vegan goodness!

Ingredients:

- 1 sheet vegan puff pastry
- 2 cups mixed vegetables (carrots, peas, potatoes, etc.), cooked
- 1 cup cooked chickpeas
- 1/2 cup diced onion
- 1/2 cup vegetable broth
- 1/2 cup unsweetened almond milk
- 2 cloves garlic, minced
- 2 tbsp all-purpose flour
- 2 tbsp vegan butter
- 1 tsp dried thyme
- Salt and pepper to taste

Directions

1. Preheat oven to 375°F (190°C).
2. In a pan, melt vegan butter and sauté diced onion and minced garlic until tender.
3. Stir in all-purpose flour and cook for 1-2 minutes.
4. Gradually add vegetable broth and almond milk, stirring constantly until the mixture thickens.
5. Stir in cooked mixed vegetables, chickpeas, dried thyme, salt, and pepper.
6. Roll out vegan puff pastry and cut into squares.
7. Divide the vegetable mixture into four ramekins.
8. Top each ramekin with a square of puff pastry.
9. Bake for 20-25 minutes until the pastry is golden and the filling is bubbly.
10. Enjoy the comforting Vegan Pot Pie!

Substitutions

None

4
servings

340
calories

45 mins

Vegan Goulash

A hearty and flavorful goulash with vegan flair!

Ingredients:

- 8 oz macaroni or pasta of your choice, cooked and drained
- 1 cup diced onion
- 1 cup diced bell peppers (assorted colors)
- 1 cup diced tomatoes
- 1 cup cooked lentils
- 1/4 cup tomato paste
- 2 cloves garlic, minced
- 2 tbsp paprika
- 1 tsp dried thyme
- Salt and pepper to taste

Directions

1. In a pan, sauté diced onion and minced garlic until tender.
2. Stir in diced bell peppers, diced tomatoes, cooked lentils, tomato paste, paprika, dried thyme, salt, and pepper.
3. Simmer for 10 minutes until heated through.
4. Add cooked pasta and toss to combine.
5. Enjoy the hearty Vegan Goulash!

Substitutions

None

4 servings

380 calories

50 mins

Vegan Cornbread and Chili

A classic pairing of vegan chili and cornbread!

Ingredients:

- 2 cups vegan chili (store-bought or homemade)
- 1 cup cornmeal
- 1 cup all-purpose flour
- 1/4 cup sugar
- 2 tsp baking powder
- 1/2 tsp baking soda
- 1/2 tsp salt
- 1 cup unsweetened almond milk
- 1/4 cup unsweetened applesauce
- 1/4 cup vegan butter, melted
- 2 tbsp maple syrup
- 1 tsp apple cider vinegar
- Vegan sour cream for serving (optional)

Substitutions

None

Directions

1. Preheat oven to 375°F (190°C).
2. In a bowl, combine cornmeal, all-purpose flour, sugar, baking powder, baking soda, and salt.
3. In another bowl, whisk together almond milk, applesauce, melted vegan butter, maple syrup, and apple cider vinegar.
4. Pour the wet ingredients into the dry ingredients and stir until just combined.
5. Pour the cornbread batter into a greased baking dish.
6. Bake for 25-30 minutes until golden.
7. Serve with heated vegan chili and a dollop of vegan sour cream if desired.
8. Enjoy the classic Vegan Cornbread and Chili duo!

4 servings | 320 calories | 30 mins

Vegan Fettuccine Alfredo

Creamy and indulgent fettuccine Alfredo, made vegan!

Ingredients:

- 8 oz fettuccine pasta, cooked and drained
- 2 cups cauliflower florets, steamed
- 1 cup unsweetened almond milk
- 1/4 cup nutritional yeast
- 2 cloves garlic, minced
- 2 tbsp vegan butter
- 1 tbsp lemon juice
- 1 tsp garlic powder
- 1/2 tsp salt
- 1/4 tsp black pepper

Directions

1. In a blender, combine steamed cauliflower florets, almond milk, nutritional yeast, minced garlic, vegan butter, lemon juice, garlic powder, salt, and black pepper.
2. Blend until smooth and creamy.
3. Pour the cauliflower Alfredo sauce over cooked fettuccine pasta.
4. Toss to combine and heat gently if needed.
5. Enjoy the creamy Vegan Fettuccine Alfredo!

Substitutions

None

Chapter 7
Tasty Tidbits

4
servings

150
calories

30 mins

Vegan Stuffed Mushrooms

Bite-sized mushrooms filled with savory vegan goodness!

Ingredients:

- 16 large mushrooms, cleaned and stems removed
- 1 cup vegan cream cheese
- 1/2 cup vegan mozzarella cheese, shredded
- 1/4 cup diced red bell pepper
- 1/4 cup chopped fresh parsley
- 2 cloves garlic, minced
- 1 tbsp olive oil
- Salt and pepper to taste

Directions

1. Preheat oven to 375°F (190°C).
2. In a bowl, mix together vegan cream cheese, vegan mozzarella cheese, diced red bell pepper, chopped fresh parsley, minced garlic, salt, and pepper.
3. Stuff each mushroom cap with the cheese mixture.
4. Place stuffed mushrooms on a baking sheet.
5. Drizzle with olive oil.
6. Bake for 20-25 minutes until mushrooms are tender and filling is bubbly.
7. Enjoy the Vegan Stuffed Mushrooms!

Substitutions

None

4 servings | 230 calories | 30 mins

Vegan Onion Rings

Crispy and golden onion rings, made vegan and delicious!

Ingredients:

- 2 large onions, cut into rings
- 1 cup all-purpose flour
- 1 cup unsweetened almond milk
- 1 cup breadcrumbs (vegan)
- 1 tsp paprika
- 1 tsp garlic powder
- Salt and pepper to taste
- Cooking oil for frying

Directions

1. Heat cooking oil in a deep fryer or a large pot to 350°F (180°C).
2. In a bowl, whisk together all-purpose flour, unsweetened almond milk, paprika, garlic powder, salt, and pepper to create a batter.
3. Dip onion rings into the batter, allowing excess to drip off.
4. Coat onion rings with breadcrumbs.
5. Fry in batches until golden brown and crispy, about 3-4 minutes per batch.
6. Remove and drain on paper towels.
7. Enjoy the Vegan Onion Rings with your favorite dipping sauce!

Substitutions

None

4
servings

180
calories

30 mins

Vegan Jalapeño Poppers

Spicy and creamy jalapeño poppers with a vegan twist!

Ingredients:

- 8 large jalapeño peppers, halved and seeds removed
- 1 cup vegan cream cheese
- 1 cup vegan cheddar cheese, shredded
- 1/2 cup breadcrumbs (vegan)
- 1/2 tsp garlic powder
- 1/2 tsp onion powder
- Salt and pepper to taste

Directions

1. Preheat oven to 375°F (190°C).
2. In a bowl, mix together vegan cream cheese, vegan cheddar cheese, garlic powder, onion powder, salt, and pepper.
3. Stuff each jalapeño half with the cheese mixture.
4. Roll the stuffed jalapeños in breadcrumbs to coat.
5. Place on a baking sheet.
6. Bake for 20-25 minutes until jalapeños are tender and breadcrumbs are golden.
7. Enjoy the Vegan Jalapeño Poppers with a cool dip!

Substitutions

None

4 servings | 320 calories | 20 mins

Vegan Loaded Nachos

A mountain of nachos piled high with vegan toppings!

Ingredients:

- 1 bag of tortilla chips (check for vegan ingredients)
- 1 cup vegan cheddar cheese, shredded
- 1 cup black beans, drained and rinsed
- 1 cup diced tomatoes
- 1/2 cup sliced black olives
- 1/2 cup sliced jalapeños
- 1/4 cup chopped fresh cilantro
- 1/4 cup diced red onion
- 1/4 cup vegan sour cream
- 1/4 cup guacamole
- 1/4 cup salsa

Directions

1. Preheat oven to 350°F (175°C).
2. Spread tortilla chips on a large baking sheet.
3. Sprinkle vegan cheddar cheese evenly over the chips.
4. Top with black beans, diced tomatoes, black olives, sliced jalapeños, chopped fresh cilantro, and diced red onion.
5. Bake for 10-15 minutes until cheese is melted.
6. Remove from the oven and drizzle with vegan sour cream, guacamole, and salsa.
7. Enjoy the loaded Vegan Nachos!

Substitutions

None

4 servings | 180 calories | 30 mins

Vegan Spinach and Artichoke Dip

A creamy and cheesy dip filled with spinach and artichokes!

Ingredients:

- 1 cup frozen chopped spinach, thawed and drained
- 1 cup canned artichoke hearts, drained and chopped
- 1 cup vegan cream cheese
- 1/2 cup vegan mayonnaise
- 1/2 cup vegan mozzarella cheese, shredded
- 1/4 cup nutritional yeast
- 2 cloves garlic, minced
- 1/2 tsp salt
- 1/4 tsp black pepper
- 1/4 tsp red pepper flakes (optional)

Directions

1. Preheat oven to 375°F (190°C).
2. In a bowl, mix together thawed and drained chopped spinach, chopped artichoke hearts, vegan cream cheese, vegan mayonnaise, vegan mozzarella cheese, nutritional yeast, minced garlic, salt, pepper, and red pepper flakes if desired.
3. Transfer the mixture to a baking dish.
4. Bake for 20-25 minutes until hot and bubbly.
5. Serve with tortilla chips or fresh veggies for dipping.
6. Enjoy the Vegan Spinach and Artichoke Dip!

Substitutions

None

4 servings | 160 calories | 30 mins

Vegan Buffalo Cauliflower Pizza Bites

Spicy and tangy cauliflower bites on a pizza crust!

Ingredients:

- 1 cauliflower head, cut into florets
- 1/2 cup buffalo sauce (vegan)
- 1 pizza dough (store-bought or homemade)
- 1/4 cup vegan ranch dressing
- 1/4 cup chopped fresh cilantro (optional)

Substitutions

None

Directions

1. Preheat oven to 450°F (230°C).
2. Toss cauliflower florets in buffalo sauce until well coated.
3. Spread the cauliflower on a baking sheet and roast for 20-25 minutes until tender and slightly crispy.
4. While the cauliflower is roasting, roll out the pizza dough into bite-sized rounds or squares.
5. Remove the cauliflower from the oven and reduce the temperature to the recommended pizza dough baking temperature.
6. Top each pizza bite with roasted cauliflower.
7. Bake according to the pizza dough instructions until the crust is golden.
8. Drizzle with vegan ranch dressing and sprinkle with chopped fresh cilantro if desired.
9. Enjoy the Vegan Buffalo Cauliflower Pizza Bites!

4 servings

210 calories

35 mins

Vegan Mozzarella Sticks

Crispy on the outside, gooey on the inside, and vegan!

Ingredients:

- 1 cup vegan mozzarella cheese, cut into sticks
- 1/2 cup all-purpose flour
- 1/2 cup unsweetened almond milk
- 1 cup breadcrumbs (vegan)
- 1 tsp garlic powder
- 1 tsp dried basil
- 1/2 tsp dried oregano
- Cooking oil for frying
- Marinara sauce for dipping

Substitutions

None

Directions

1. Freeze the vegan mozzarella sticks for at least 30 minutes.
2. In a bowl, whisk together all-purpose flour and unsweetened almond milk to create a batter.
3. In another bowl, combine breadcrumbs, garlic powder, dried basil, and dried oregano.
4. Dip each frozen mozzarella stick into the batter, allowing excess to drip off, then coat in the breadcrumb mixture.
5. Repeat the dipping and coating process for a thicker breading.
6. Place the coated mozzarella sticks on a baking sheet and freeze for an additional 30 minutes.
7. Heat cooking oil to 350°F (180°C) in a deep fryer or large pot.
8. Fry the frozen mozzarella sticks until golden brown, about 3-4 minutes.
9. Remove and drain on paper towels.
10. Serve with marinara sauce for dipping.
11. Enjoy the Vegan Mozzarella Sticks, hot and melty!

4 servings | 320 calories | 40 mins

Vegan Chili Cheese Fries

A tower of crispy fries smothered in vegan chili and cheese!

Ingredients:

- 4 cups frozen French fries (check for vegan ingredients)
- 2 cups vegan chili (store-bought or homemade)
- 1 cup vegan cheddar cheese, shredded
- 1/2 cup diced red onion
- 1/4 cup sliced jalapeños
- 1/4 cup chopped fresh cilantro
- Vegan sour cream for dipping (optional)

Directions

1. Bake frozen French fries according to package instructions until crispy.
2. While the fries are baking, heat the vegan chili on the stove or in the microwave.
3. Once the fries are ready, transfer them to a serving platter.
4. Pour hot vegan chili over the fries.
5. Sprinkle vegan cheddar cheese, diced red onion, sliced jalapeños, and chopped fresh cilantro on top.
6. Serve with vegan sour cream for dipping if desired.
7. Enjoy the indulgent Vegan Chili Cheese Fries!

Substitutions

None

4 servings | 120 calories | 20 mins

Easy

Vegan Bruschetta

Fresh and vibrant bruschetta with a vegan twist!

Ingredients:

- 4 slices of baguette or Italian bread
- 2 cups diced tomatoes
- 1/4 cup chopped fresh basil
- 2 cloves garlic, minced
- 2 tbsp extra-virgin olive oil
- 1 tbsp balsamic vinegar
- Salt and pepper to taste

Directions

1. Preheat oven to 375°F (190°C).
2. Place bread slices on a baking sheet and toast for 5-7 minutes until lightly golden.
3. In a bowl, combine diced tomatoes, chopped fresh basil, minced garlic, extra-virgin olive oil, balsamic vinegar, salt, and pepper.
4. Spoon the tomato mixture onto the toasted bread slices.
5. Serve immediately, and savor the freshness of Vegan Bruschetta!

Substitutions

None

4 servings | 180 calories | 35 mins

Vegan Garlic Knots

Soft and garlicky knots of deliciousness, vegan style!

Ingredients:

- 1 package of store-bought pizza dough (check for vegan ingredients)
- 1/4 cup vegan butter, melted
- 2 cloves garlic, minced
- 2 tbsp chopped fresh parsley
- Salt to taste

Directions

1. Preheat oven according to the pizza dough package instructions.
2. Roll out the pizza dough into a rectangle on a floured surface.
3. Cut the dough into strips and tie each strip into a knot.
4. Place the knots on a baking sheet lined with parchment paper.
5. Bake according to the pizza dough instructions until golden brown.
6. While the knots are baking, mix melted vegan butter, minced garlic, chopped fresh parsley, and a pinch of salt in a bowl.
7. Brush the garlic butter mixture over the hot knots as soon as they come out of the oven.
8. Enjoy the soft and garlicky Vegan Garlic Knots!

Substitutions

None

Chapter 8
Savory Wraps

1 wrap

350 calories

15 mins

Vegan BBQ Wrap

Smoky BBQ flavors wrapped in a delightful vegan package!

Ingredients:

- 1 large tortilla (check for vegan ingredients)
- 1/2 cup vegan BBQ sauce
- 1/2 cup cooked chickpeas
- 1/2 cup sliced bell peppers
- 1/4 cup sliced red onion
- 1/4 cup shredded lettuce
- 1/4 cup shredded carrots
- 1/4 cup corn kernels
- 1/4 cup chopped fresh cilantro
- Vegan ranch dressing for drizzling (optional)

Directions

1. Lay out the tortilla on a clean surface.
2. Spread a layer of vegan BBQ sauce over the tortilla.
3. Add cooked chickpeas, sliced bell peppers, sliced red onion, shredded lettuce, shredded carrots, corn kernels, and chopped fresh cilantro on top of the BBQ sauce.
4. Drizzle with vegan ranch dressing if desired.
5. Fold in the sides of the tortilla and then roll it up tightly.
6. Slice in half if you prefer.
7. Enjoy the Vegan BBQ Wrap!

Substitutions

None

1 wrap

320 calories

15 mins

Vegan Mediterranean Wrap

A taste of the Mediterranean in a satisfying vegan wrap!

Ingredients:

- 1 large tortilla (check for vegan ingredients)
- 1/2 cup hummus
- 1/2 cup diced cucumber
- 1/2 cup diced tomatoes
- 1/4 cup sliced black olives
- 1/4 cup sliced red onion
- 1/4 cup chopped fresh parsley
- 2 tbsp lemon juice
- Salt and pepper to taste

Directions

1. Lay out the tortilla on a clean surface.
2. Spread a layer of hummus over the tortilla.
3. Add diced cucumber, diced tomatoes, sliced black olives, sliced red onion, chopped fresh parsley, lemon juice, salt, and pepper on top of the hummus.
4. Fold in the sides of the tortilla and then roll it up tightly.
5. Slice in half if you prefer.
6. Enjoy the Vegan Mediterranean Wrap!

Substitutions

None

1 wrap

380 calories

20 mins

Vegan Teriyaki Wrap

Sweet and savory teriyaki flavors in a vegan wrap!

Ingredients:

- 1 large tortilla (check for vegan ingredients)
- 1/2 cup cooked tofu or tempeh, sliced
- 1/2 cup cooked brown rice
- 1/4 cup sliced bell peppers
- 1/4 cup sliced pineapple
- 1/4 cup sliced red cabbage
- 1/4 cup sliced cucumber
- 2 tbsp teriyaki sauce (vegan)
- Sesame seeds for garnish (optional)

Substitutions

None

Directions

1. Lay out the tortilla on a clean surface.
2. Arrange cooked tofu or tempeh slices and cooked brown rice over the tortilla.
3. Add sliced bell peppers, sliced pineapple, sliced red cabbage, and sliced cucumber on top.
4. Drizzle with vegan teriyaki sauce.
5. Sprinkle with sesame seeds if desired.
6. Fold in the sides of the tortilla and then roll it up tightly.
7. Slice in half if you prefer.
8. Enjoy the Vegan Teriyaki Wrap!

1 wrap

320 calories

15 mins

Vegan Caesar Wrap

Creamy Caesar dressing enveloping crisp veggies, vegan-style!

Ingredients:

- 1 large tortilla (check for vegan ingredients)
- 1/2 cup sliced vegan chicken strips (store-bought or homemade)
- 1/2 cup chopped romaine lettuce
- 1/4 cup sliced cherry tomatoes
- 1/4 cup vegan Caesar dressing
- 2 tbsp vegan Parmesan cheese
- Salt and pepper to taste

Directions

1. Lay out the tortilla on a clean surface.
2. Arrange sliced vegan chicken strips, chopped romaine lettuce, and sliced cherry tomatoes over the tortilla.
3. Drizzle with vegan Caesar dressing.
4. Sprinkle with vegan Parmesan cheese, salt, and pepper.
5. Fold in the sides of the tortilla and then roll it up tightly.
6. Slice in half if you prefer.
7. Enjoy the Vegan Caesar Wrap!

Substitutions

None

1 wrap

300 calories

15 mins

Vegan Chickpea Salad Wrap

A hearty and protein-packed chickpea salad wrapped in vegan goodness!

Ingredients:

- 1 large tortilla (check for vegan ingredients)
- 1/2 cup mashed chickpeas
- 1/4 cup diced cucumber
- 1/4 cup diced bell peppers
- 1/4 cup diced red onion
- 2 tbsp vegan mayonnaise
- 1 tbsp Dijon mustard
- 1 tsp lemon juice
- 1/2 tsp garlic powder
- Salt and pepper to taste

Directions

1. Lay out the tortilla on a clean surface.
2. In a bowl, mix together mashed chickpeas, diced cucumber, diced bell peppers, diced red onion, vegan mayonnaise, Dijon mustard, lemon juice, garlic powder, salt, and pepper.
3. Spread the chickpea salad mixture over the tortilla.
4. Fold in the sides of the tortilla and then roll it up tightly.
5. Slice in half if you prefer.
6. Enjoy the Vegan Chickpea Salad Wrap!

Substitutions

None

1 wrap

360 calories

20 mins

Vegan Falafel Wrap

Crispy falafel, fresh veggies, and tahini in a vegan wrap!

Ingredients:

- 1 large tortilla (check for vegan ingredients)
- 4 vegan falafel patties (store-bought or homemade)
- 1/4 cup diced cucumber
- 1/4 cup diced tomatoes
- 1/4 cup diced red onion
- 1/4 cup shredded lettuce
- 2 tbsp tahini sauce (vegan)
- 1 tbsp lemon juice
- Salt and pepper to taste

Substitutions

None

Directions

1. Lay out the tortilla on a clean surface.
2. Warm the falafel patties according to the package instructions or cook homemade falafel.
3. Arrange falafel patties, diced cucumber, diced tomatoes, diced red onion, shredded lettuce, tahini sauce, lemon juice, salt, and pepper over the tortilla.
4. Fold in the sides of the tortilla and then roll it up tightly.
5. Slice in half if you prefer.
6. Enjoy the Vegan Falafel Wrap!

1 wrap

340 calories

15 mins

Vegan Club Wrap

A vegan twist on the classic club sandwich, wrapped for convenience!

Ingredients:

- 1 large tortilla (check for vegan ingredients)
- 1/2 cup sliced vegan turkey or smoked tofu
- 1/4 cup sliced avocado
- 1/4 cup sliced tomato
- 1/4 cup shredded lettuce
- 2 tbsp vegan mayonnaise
- 1 tsp Dijon mustard
- Salt and pepper to taste

Directions

1. Lay out the tortilla on a clean surface.
2. Arrange sliced vegan turkey or smoked tofu, sliced avocado, sliced tomato, shredded lettuce, vegan mayonnaise, Dijon mustard, salt, and pepper over the tortilla.
3. Fold in the sides of the tortilla and then roll it up tightly.
4. Slice in half if you prefer.
5. Enjoy the Vegan Club Wrap!

Substitutions

None

1 wrap

330 calories

15 mins

Vegan California Wrap

Fresh and vibrant California-inspired vegan wrap!

Ingredients:

- 1 large tortilla (check for vegan ingredients)
- 1/2 cup sliced avocado
- 1/4 cup sliced cucumber
- 1/4 cup sliced bell peppers
- 1/4 cup sliced red onion
- 1/4 cup shredded lettuce
- 2 tbsp vegan ranch dressing
- 1 tbsp lemon juice
- Salt and pepper to taste

Directions

1. Lay out the tortilla on a clean surface.
2. Arrange sliced avocado, sliced cucumber, sliced bell peppers, sliced red onion, shredded lettuce, vegan ranch dressing, lemon juice, salt, and pepper over the tortilla.
3. Fold in the sides of the tortilla and then roll it up tightly.
4. Slice in half if you prefer.
5. Enjoy the Vegan California Wrap!

Substitutions

None

1 wrap

340 calories

25 mins

Vegan Tofu Satay Wrap

Creamy peanut satay tofu wrapped in vegan deliciousness!

Ingredients:

- 1 large tortilla (check for vegan ingredients)
- 1/2 cup cubed tofu, cooked
- 1/4 cup sliced cucumber
- 1/4 cup shredded carrot
- 1/4 cup chopped fresh cilantro
- 2 tbsp peanut satay sauce (vegan)
- 1 tbsp lime juice
- Salt and pepper to taste

Directions

1. Lay out the tortilla on a clean surface.
2. Arrange cooked tofu cubes, sliced cucumber, shredded carrot, chopped fresh cilantro, peanut satay sauce, lime juice, salt, and pepper over the tortilla.
3. Fold in the sides of the tortilla and then roll it up tightly.
4. Slice in half if you prefer.
5. Enjoy the Vegan Tofu Satay Wrap!

Substitutions

None

1 wrap

280 calories

20 mins

Vegan Spinach and Mushroom Wrap

Sautéed spinach and mushrooms wrapped in a delightful vegan package!

Ingredients:

- 1 large tortilla (check for vegan ingredients)
- 1 cup fresh spinach
- 1 cup sliced mushrooms
- 1/4 cup sliced red onion
- 1/4 cup sliced bell peppers
- 2 tbsp vegan cream cheese
- 1 tbsp balsamic vinegar
- Salt and pepper to taste

Directions

1. Lay out the tortilla on a clean surface.
2. In a pan, sauté fresh spinach, sliced mushrooms, sliced red onion, and sliced bell peppers until tender.
3. Stir in vegan cream cheese, balsamic vinegar, salt, and pepper.
4. Transfer the sautéed mixture onto the tortilla.
5. Fold in the sides of the tortilla and then roll it up tightly.
6. Slice in half if you prefer.
7. Enjoy the Vegan Spinach and Mushroom Wrap!

Substitutions

None

Chapter 9
Creative Creations

4 servings | 250 calories | 35 mins

Vegan Jackfruit Tacos

Tangy and savory jackfruit tacos for a fiesta!

Ingredients:

- 1 can young green jackfruit in brine, drained and shredded
- 1 cup diced onion
- 1/2 cup diced bell peppers
- 1/2 cup canned black beans, drained and rinsed
- 1/4 cup tomato paste
- 2 cloves garlic, minced
- 2 tbsp taco seasoning
- 1 tbsp lime juice
- Salt and pepper to taste
- 8 small taco shells (check for vegan ingredients)
- Toppings: diced tomatoes, shredded lettuce, vegan cheese, vegan sour cream, and salsa

Substitutions

None

Directions

1. In a pan, sauté shredded jackfruit, diced onion, and diced bell peppers until softened.
2. Add canned black beans, tomato paste, minced garlic, taco seasoning, lime juice, salt, and pepper. Stir well.
3. Cook for an additional 5 minutes, allowing flavors to meld.
4. Warm taco shells in the oven according to package instructions.
5. Fill taco shells with the jackfruit mixture.
6. Top with diced tomatoes, shredded lettuce, vegan cheese, vegan sour cream, and salsa.
7. Enjoy the Vegan Jackfruit Tacos!

2
servings

320
calories

30 mins

Vegan Kimchi Ramen

Spicy and savory kimchi ramen with a vegan twist!

Ingredients:

- 6 oz vegan ramen noodles
- 2 cups vegetable broth
- 1 cup kimchi, chopped
- 1/2 cup sliced shiitake mushrooms
- 1/4 cup diced tofu
- 2 cloves garlic, minced
- 1 tbsp soy sauce (vegan)
- 1 tbsp sesame oil
- 1 tsp gochugaru (Korean red pepper flakes)
- Green onions for garnish
- Sesame seeds for garnish

Directions

1. Cook vegan ramen noodles according to package instructions, then drain and set aside.
2. In a pot, bring vegetable broth to a simmer.
3. Add chopped kimchi, sliced shiitake mushrooms, diced tofu, minced garlic, soy sauce, sesame oil, and gochugaru.
4. Simmer for 15-20 minutes to meld flavors.
5. Divide cooked ramen noodles into bowls.
6. Ladle the kimchi broth over the noodles.
7. Garnish with green onions and sesame seeds.
8. Enjoy the Vegan Kimchi Ramen!

Substitutions

None

2
servings

290
calories

30 mins

Vegan Portobello Steak Sandwich

Hearty Portobello steak sandwich, vegan-style!

Ingredients:

- 2 large Portobello mushrooms, stems removed
- 2 large sandwich rolls (check for vegan ingredients)
- 1/4 cup sliced red onion
- 1/4 cup sliced bell peppers
- 1/4 cup baby spinach
- 2 tbsp balsamic vinegar
- 1 tbsp olive oil
- 1 tsp garlic powder
- Salt and pepper to taste

Substitutions

None

Directions

1. Preheat grill or grill pan over medium-high heat.
2. In a bowl, whisk together balsamic vinegar, olive oil, garlic powder, salt, and pepper.
3. Brush the Portobello mushrooms with the balsamic mixture.
4. Grill the mushrooms for about 5-7 minutes per side until tender.
5. While grilling, toast the sandwich rolls on the grill.
6. Assemble the sandwiches with grilled Portobello mushrooms, sliced red onion, sliced bell peppers, and baby spinach.
7. Enjoy the Vegan Portobello Steak Sandwich!

4 servings

280 calories

35 mins

Vegan Sweet and Sour Tempeh

A balance of sweet and sour with tempeh goodness!

Ingredients:

- 8 oz tempeh, cubed
- 1 cup pineapple chunks (canned or fresh)
- 1/2 cup diced bell peppers
- 1/2 cup diced onion
- 1/4 cup pineapple juice (from canned pineapple)
- 2 tbsp soy sauce (vegan)
- 2 tbsp rice vinegar
- 2 tbsp ketchup (vegan)
- 1 tbsp brown sugar
- 1 tsp cornstarch
- 1 tsp ginger, minced
- 1 tsp garlic, minced
- Cooking oil for sautéing
- Cooked rice for serving

Substitutions

None

Directions

1. In a bowl, whisk together pineapple juice, soy sauce, rice vinegar, ketchup, brown sugar, and cornstarch. Set aside.
2. In a pan, heat cooking oil over medium-high heat.
3. Sauté tempeh cubes until golden brown. Remove and set aside.
4. In the same pan, add a bit more oil if needed and sauté diced onion, diced bell peppers, minced ginger, and minced garlic until softened.
5. Add pineapple chunks and cooked tempeh to the pan.
6. Pour the sweet and sour sauce over the tempeh mixture.
7. Cook and stir until the sauce thickens and coats everything, about 2-3 minutes.
8. Serve over cooked rice.
9. Enjoy the Vegan Sweet and Sour Tempeh!

4 servings

350 calories

40 mins

Vegan Coconut Curry with Tofu

Creamy coconut curry with tofu for a satisfying meal!

Ingredients:

- 14 oz firm tofu, cubed
- 1 can (14 oz) coconut milk
- 1 cup vegetable broth
- 1/2 cup diced bell peppers
- 1/2 cup diced onion
- 1/2 cup sliced carrots
- 1/4 cup frozen peas
- 2 cloves garlic, minced
- 2 tbsp red curry paste
- 1 tbsp soy sauce (vegan)
- 1 tbsp brown sugar
- 1 tbsp vegetable oil
- Salt and pepper to taste
- Cooked rice for serving

Substitutions

None

Directions

1. In a large pan, heat vegetable oil over medium-high heat.
2. Sauté cubed tofu until golden brown on all sides. Remove and set aside.
3. In the same pan, sauté diced onion, diced bell peppers, sliced carrots, minced garlic, and frozen peas until softened.
4. Stir in red curry paste and sauté for another minute.
5. Add coconut milk, vegetable broth, soy sauce, brown sugar, salt, and pepper. Stir well.
6. Return the sautéed tofu to the pan and simmer for 10-15 minutes to meld flavors.
7. Serve over cooked rice.
8. Enjoy the Vegan Coconut Curry with Tofu!

4 servings | 220 calories | 30 mins

Vegan BBQ Cauliflower Tacos

Smoky BBQ cauliflower tucked into soft taco shells!

Ingredients:

- 1 small cauliflower head, cut into florets
- 1 cup BBQ sauce (vegan)
- 1/2 cup diced red onion
- 1/2 cup diced pineapple
- 1/4 cup chopped fresh cilantro
- 1/4 cup vegan coleslaw
- 8 small taco shells (check for vegan ingredients)

Substitutions

None

Directions

1. Preheat oven to 425°F (220°C).
2. Toss cauliflower florets in BBQ sauce until well coated.
3. Spread the cauliflower on a baking sheet and roast for 20-25 minutes until tender and slightly crispy.
4. Warm taco shells in the oven according to package instructions.
5. Fill taco shells with BBQ cauliflower, diced red onion, diced pineapple, chopped fresh cilantro, and vegan coleslaw.
6. Enjoy the Vegan BBQ Cauliflower Tacos!

2 servings

340 calories

35 mins

Fiery jerk tofu with Caribbean flavors in a sandwich!

Vegan Jerk Tofu Sandwich

Ingredients:

- 8 oz extra-firm tofu, sliced
- 2 large sandwich rolls (check for vegan ingredients)
- 1/4 cup sliced red onion
- 1/4 cup sliced bell peppers
- 1/4 cup sliced pineapple
- 2 tbsp jerk seasoning (vegan)
- 1 tbsp olive oil
- 1 tbsp lime juice
- Salt and pepper to taste

Directions

1. In a bowl, mix jerk seasoning, olive oil, lime juice, salt, and pepper.
2. Marinate tofu slices in the jerk mixture for at least 15 minutes.
3. Grill or pan-fry tofu until it's heated through and has grill marks, about 3-4 minutes per side.
4. While tofu is cooking, toast the sandwich rolls.
5. Assemble sandwiches with grilled jerk tofu, sliced red onion, sliced bell peppers, and sliced pineapple.
6. Enjoy the Vegan Jerk Tofu Sandwich!

Substitutions

None

2 servings | 320 calories | 40 mins

Vegan Teriyaki Eggplant Burger

Juicy teriyaki-glazed eggplant burger with vegan flair!

Ingredients:

- 2 large burger buns (check for vegan ingredients)
- 1 large eggplant, sliced into rounds
- 1/2 cup teriyaki sauce (vegan)
- 1/4 cup sliced cucumber
- 1/4 cup shredded carrot
- 1/4 cup sliced red onion
- 2 tbsp vegan mayonnaise
- 1 tbsp soy sauce (vegan)
- 1 tbsp vegetable oil
- Salt and pepper to taste

Substitutions

None

Directions

1. Preheat grill or grill pan over medium-high heat.
2. Brush eggplant slices with vegetable oil and season with salt and pepper.
3. Grill eggplant slices for about 3-4 minutes per side until tender and grill marks appear.
4. In a bowl, whisk together teriyaki sauce and soy sauce.
5. Brush the grilled eggplant with the teriyaki mixture.
6. Grill for an additional 1-2 minutes per side to glaze.
7. Toast burger buns on the grill.
8. Assemble burgers with glazed eggplant slices, sliced cucumber, shredded carrot, and sliced red onion.
9. Spread vegan mayonnaise on the buns.
10. Enjoy the Vegan Teriyaki Eggplant Burger!

4 servings | 320 calories | 30 mins

Easy

Vegan Thai Pineapple Fried Rice

Fragrant Thai pineapple fried rice, now vegan!

Ingredients:

- 2 cups cooked jasmine rice, chilled
- 1 cup diced pineapple
- 1/2 cup diced bell peppers
- 1/2 cup diced carrot
- 1/2 cup frozen peas
- 1/4 cup sliced green onions
- 1/4 cup chopped fresh cilantro
- 2 tbsp soy sauce (vegan)
- 2 tbsp vegetable oil
- 1 tbsp red curry paste
- 1 tsp brown sugar
- 1/2 tsp turmeric powder
- 1/2 tsp garlic powder
- 1/2 tsp ginger powder
- Salt and pepper to taste

Substitutions

None

Directions

1. In a pan, heat vegetable oil over medium-high heat.
2. Sauté diced bell peppers, diced carrot, and frozen peas until slightly softened.
3. Stir in red curry paste, turmeric powder, garlic powder, and ginger powder.
4. Add chilled cooked jasmine rice and diced pineapple to the pan. Stir-fry for 3-4 minutes until heated through.
5. Drizzle soy sauce and sprinkle brown sugar, salt, and pepper over the rice. Stir well.
6. Stir in sliced green onions and chopped fresh cilantro.
7. Serve the Vegan Thai Pineapple Fried Rice hot.
8. Enjoy!

4 servings

180 calories

20 mins

Vegan BLT Salad

Crisp and savory salad with a vegan BLT twist!

Ingredients:

- 6 cups mixed greens
- 1 cup cherry tomatoes, halved
- 1/2 cup diced cucumber
- 1/4 cup vegan bacon bits (store-bought or homemade)
- 1/4 cup croutons (check for vegan ingredients)
- 1/4 cup vegan ranch dressing
- 1 tbsp chopped fresh chives
- Salt and pepper to taste

Directions

1. In a large salad bowl, combine mixed greens, cherry tomatoes, diced cucumber, vegan bacon bits, and croutons.
2. Drizzle vegan ranch dressing over the salad.
3. Toss everything together until well coated.
4. Garnish with chopped fresh chives, salt, and pepper.
5. Serve the Vegan BLT Salad as a side or a light meal.
6. Enjoy!

Substitutions

None

Chapter 10

Hearty Breakfast All Day

4
servings

320
calories

35 mins

Vegan Breakfast Pizza

A morning delight, pizza-style, with a vegan twist!

Ingredients:

- 1 pizza crust (check for vegan ingredients)
- 1/2 cup vegan breakfast sausage crumbles (store-bought or homemade)
- 1/2 cup vegan shredded cheddar cheese
- 1/4 cup diced bell peppers
- 1/4 cup diced onion
- 1/4 cup sliced mushrooms
- 1/4 cup sliced black olives
- 1/4 cup tomato sauce
- 1/2 tsp dried oregano
- Salt and pepper to taste

Directions

1. Preheat the oven according to the pizza crust package instructions.
2. Roll out the pizza crust on a baking sheet or pizza stone.
3. Spread tomato sauce evenly over the crust.
4. Sprinkle vegan breakfast sausage crumbles, vegan shredded cheddar cheese, diced bell peppers, diced onion, sliced mushrooms, sliced black olives, dried oregano, salt, and pepper over the sauce.
5. Bake in the preheated oven as per the crust instructions until the crust is golden and the cheese is bubbly.
6. Slice and enjoy the Vegan Breakfast Pizza!

Substitutions

None

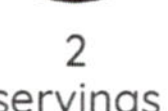

2 servings | 280 calories | 20 mins

Vegan Breakfast Quesadilla

A cheesy and savory breakfast quesadilla, vegan-style!

Ingredients:

- 2 large flour tortillas (check for vegan ingredients)
- 1/2 cup vegan scrambled eggs
- 1/4 cup vegan shredded cheddar cheese
- 1/4 cup diced bell peppers
- 1/4 cup diced onion
- 1/4 cup chopped fresh spinach
- 2 tbsp salsa (check for vegan ingredients)
- 1 tsp olive oil
- Salt and pepper to taste

Substitutions

None

Directions

1. In a pan, heat olive oil over medium-high heat.
2. Sauté diced bell peppers and diced onion until softened.
3. Remove from the pan and set aside.
4. Place one tortilla in the pan and spread vegan shredded cheddar cheese, sautéed bell peppers and onion, chopped fresh spinach, and vegan scrambled eggs on top.
5. Place the second tortilla on top.
6. Cook until the bottom tortilla is golden and crispy, then carefully flip to cook the other side.
7. Remove from the pan, slice, and serve with salsa.
8. Enjoy the Vegan Breakfast Quesadilla!

2 servings

340 calories

20 mins

Vegan Breakfast Sausage Sandwich

A hearty breakfast sandwich featuring vegan sausage!

Ingredients:

- 2 large English muffins (check for vegan ingredients)
- 4 vegan breakfast sausage patties (store-bought or homemade)
- 2 slices vegan American cheese
- 2 vegan fried eggs (tofu or chickpea flour-based)
- 1/4 cup sliced avocado
- 2 tbsp vegan mayonnaise
- 1 tbsp ketchup (vegan)
- 1 tsp hot sauce (optional)
- Salt and pepper to taste

Substitutions

None

Directions

1. Cook vegan breakfast sausage patties according to package instructions or prepare homemade patties.
2. Toast English muffins until lightly browned.
3. In a small bowl, mix vegan mayonnaise, ketchup, hot sauce (if using), salt, and pepper to make a sauce.
4. Assemble sandwiches by placing a slice of vegan American cheese on the bottom half of each English muffin.
5. Top with a vegan sausage patty, a vegan fried egg, and sliced avocado.
6. Drizzle the sauce over the top half of the English muffins and place them on the sandwiches.
7. Serve the Vegan Breakfast Sausage Sandwiches with your favorite hot sauce if desired.
8. Enjoy!

4 servings | 240 calories | 25 mins

Vegan Breakfast Tostadas

Crispy tostadas topped with vegan breakfast goodness!

Ingredients:

- 4 tostada shells (check for vegan ingredients)
- 1 cup vegan scrambled eggs
- 1/2 cup refried black beans (canned or homemade)
- 1/4 cup diced tomato
- 1/4 cup diced avocado
- 1/4 cup chopped fresh cilantro
- 2 tbsp salsa (check for vegan ingredients)
- 1 tbsp olive oil
- Salt and pepper to taste

Directions

1. In a pan, heat olive oil over medium-high heat.
2. Warm tostada shells in the pan for a minute on each side until slightly crispy.
3. Spread refried black beans evenly on each tostada shell.
4. Top with vegan scrambled eggs, diced tomato, diced avocado, chopped fresh cilantro, salsa, salt, and pepper.
5. Serve the Vegan Breakfast Tostadas with extra salsa on the side.
6. Enjoy!

Substitutions

None

6 servings

280 calories

40 mins

Vegan Breakfast Tater Tot Casserole

A comforting tater tot casserole perfect for breakfast!

Ingredients:

- 1 lb frozen vegan tater tots
- 1 cup vegan scrambled eggs
- 1/2 cup diced bell peppers
- 1/2 cup diced onion
- 1/2 cup vegan shredded cheddar cheese
- 1/4 cup sliced black olives
- 1/4 cup diced tomatoes
- 1/4 cup chopped fresh parsley
- 2 tbsp vegan sour cream
- 1 tbsp olive oil
- Salt and pepper to taste

Directions

1. Preheat the oven to 375°F (190°C).
2. In a large ovenproof skillet or casserole dish, heat olive oil over medium-high heat.
3. Sauté diced bell peppers and diced onion until softened.
4. Remove from heat and layer the bottom with frozen vegan tater tots.
5. Top with vegan scrambled eggs, vegan shredded cheddar cheese, sliced black olives, diced tomatoes, chopped fresh parsley, salt, and pepper.
6. Bake in the preheated oven for about 30 minutes or until tater tots are golden and crispy.
7. Remove from the oven, drizzle with vegan sour cream, and serve the Vegan Breakfast Tater Tot Casserole hot.
8. Enjoy!

Substitutions

None

6 servings

220 calories

30 mins

Vegan Breakfast Sliders

Mini breakfast sliders with vegan sausage patties!

Ingredients:

- 6 small vegan slider buns (check for vegan ingredients)
- 6 vegan breakfast sausage patties (store-bought or homemade)
- 6 vegan scrambled egg patties (tofu or chickpea flour-based)
- 6 vegan American cheese slices
- 1/4 cup vegan mayonnaise
- 2 tbsp ketchup (vegan)
- 1 tsp hot sauce (optional)
- Salt and pepper to taste

Substitutions

None

Directions

1. Cook vegan breakfast sausage patties according to package instructions or prepare homemade patties.
2. Cook vegan scrambled egg patties according to your chosen recipe.
3. In a small bowl, mix vegan mayonnaise, ketchup, hot sauce (if using), salt, and pepper to make a sauce.
4. Split the slider buns and lightly toast them.
5. Assemble the sliders by placing a vegan American cheese slice on the bottom half of each bun.
6. Top with a vegan sausage patty, a vegan scrambled egg patty, and the top half of the bun.
7. Drizzle the sauce over the sliders.
8. Serve the Vegan Breakfast Sliders with your favorite hot sauce if desired.
9. Enjoy!

8 servings

260 calories

75 mins

Vegan Breakfast Tamales

Handmade tamales filled with vegan breakfast goodness!

Ingredients:

- 1 cup masa harina (corn flour for tamales)
- 3/4 cup vegetable broth
- 1/4 cup vegetable oil
- 1/2 tsp baking powder
- 1/2 tsp salt
- 1/4 tsp chili powder
- 1/4 tsp cumin
- 1/4 tsp garlic powder
- 1/4 tsp onion powder
- 1/4 tsp smoked paprika
- 1/4 cup vegan breakfast sausage crumbles (store-bought or homemade)
- 1/4 cup diced bell peppers
- 1/4 cup diced onion
- 1/4 cup vegan shredded cheddar cheese
- 1/4 cup diced tomatoes
- 1/4 cup chopped fresh cilantro
- Salt and pepper to taste

Substitutions

None

Directions

1. In a mixing bowl, combine masa harina, vegetable broth, vegetable oil, baking powder, salt, chili powder, cumin, garlic powder, onion powder, and smoked paprika. Mix until a dough forms.
2. In a pan, heat olive oil over medium-high heat.
3. Sauté diced bell peppers and diced onion until softened.
4. Remove from heat and stir in vegan breakfast sausage crumbles, vegan shredded cheddar cheese, diced tomatoes, chopped fresh cilantro, salt, and pepper.
5. Take a small handful of the masa dough and flatten it on a corn husk.
6. Spoon the breakfast filling onto the masa dough and wrap the tamale, securing the ends with a strip of corn husk.
7. Repeat for the remaining masa dough and filling.
8. Steam the tamales for 45-60 minutes until the masa is cooked through and no longer sticks to the corn husk.
9. Serve the Vegan Breakfast Tamales hot, garnished with extra cilantro if desired.
10. Enjoy!

4 servings

260 calories

35 mins

Vegan Breakfast Frittata

A fluffy and savory breakfast frittata with a vegan twist!

Ingredients:

- 1 cup vegan chickpea flour
- 1 cup water
- 1/4 cup nutritional yeast
- 1/2 tsp turmeric powder
- 1/2 tsp garlic powder
- 1/2 tsp onion powder
- Salt and pepper to taste
- 1/2 cup diced bell peppers
- 1/2 cup diced onion
- 1/2 cup diced zucchini
- 1/2 cup sliced cherry tomatoes
- 1/4 cup chopped fresh basil
- 2 tbsp olive oil

Directions

1. Preheat the oven to 375°F (190°C).
2. In a blender, combine vegan chickpea flour, water, nutritional yeast, turmeric powder, garlic powder, onion powder, salt, and pepper. Blend until smooth.
3. In an ovenproof skillet, heat olive oil over medium-high heat.
4. Sauté diced bell peppers, diced onion, and diced zucchini until slightly softened.
5. Pour the chickpea flour mixture over the sautéed vegetables.
6. Arrange sliced cherry tomatoes on top.
7. Transfer the skillet to the preheated oven and bake for 20-25 minutes until the frittata is set and golden.
8. Remove from the oven, garnish with chopped fresh basil, and let it cool slightly before slicing.
9. Serve the Vegan Breakfast Frittata warm.
10. Enjoy!

Substitutions

None

12 servings

220 calories

50 mins

Vegan Breakfast Empanadas

Flaky empanadas stuffed with vegan breakfast goodness!

Ingredients:

- 2 cups all-purpose flour
- 1/2 cup vegetable shortening or vegan butter
- 1/2 cup ice-cold water
- 1 cup vegan scrambled eggs
- 1/2 cup vegan breakfast sausage crumbles (store-bought or homemade)
- 1/4 cup diced bell peppers
- 1/4 cup diced onion
- 1/4 cup vegan shredded cheddar cheese
- 1/4 cup diced tomatoes
- 1/4 cup chopped fresh cilantro
- Salt and pepper to taste

Substitutions

None

Directions

1. In a large mixing bowl, combine all-purpose flour and vegetable shortening or vegan butter. Mix until it resembles coarse crumbs.
2. Gradually add ice-cold water and mix until a dough forms. Shape it into a ball, cover with plastic wrap, and refrigerate for 30 minutes.
3. In a pan, heat olive oil over medium-high heat.
4. Sauté diced bell peppers and diced onion until softened.
5. Remove from heat and stir in vegan breakfast sausage crumbles, vegan shredded cheddar cheese, diced tomatoes, chopped fresh cilantro, salt, and pepper.
6. Preheat the oven to 375°F (190°C).
7. Roll out the refrigerated dough on a floured surface and cut it into rounds.
8. Place a spoonful of the breakfast filling in the center of each dough round.
9. Fold the dough over to create half-moon shapes and seal the edges with a fork.
10. Transfer the empanadas to a baking sheet lined with parchment paper.
11. Bake for 20-25 minutes until golden brown.
12. Serve the Vegan Breakfast Empanadas hot or at room temperature.
13. Enjoy!

Chapter 11

Sensational Sliders

4 servings | 280 calories | 40 mins

Vegan BBQ Jackfruit Sliders

Tangy BBQ jackfruit sliders that are a crowd-pleaser!

Ingredients:

- 4 small vegan slider buns (check for vegan ingredients)
- 1 can young jackfruit in brine, drained and shredded
- 1/2 cup BBQ sauce (vegan)
- 1/4 cup sliced red onion
- 1/4 cup pickles
- 1/4 cup coleslaw (vegan)
- 1 tbsp vegetable oil
- Salt and pepper to taste

Substitutions

None

Directions

1. In a pan, heat vegetable oil over medium-high heat.
2. Add shredded jackfruit and sauté until it starts to brown.
3. Pour in BBQ sauce, salt, and pepper. Cook for an additional 5-7 minutes, stirring occasionally.
4. Split and toast slider buns until lightly browned.
5. Assemble sliders with BBQ jackfruit, sliced red onion, pickles, and coleslaw.
6. Serve the Vegan BBQ Jackfruit Sliders with extra BBQ sauce if desired.
7. Enjoy!

4 servings

240 calories

30 mins

Vegan Portobello Mushroom Sliders

Hearty Portobello mushroom sliders with savory toppings!

Ingredients:

- 4 small vegan slider buns (check for vegan ingredients)
- 4 large Portobello mushroom caps
- 1/4 cup balsamic vinegar
- 2 tbsp olive oil
- 2 cloves garlic, minced
- 1/4 cup vegan pesto
- 1/4 cup roasted red bell peppers, sliced
- 1/4 cup baby spinach leaves
- Salt and pepper to taste

Substitutions

None

Directions

1. Preheat grill or grill pan over medium-high heat.
2. In a bowl, whisk together balsamic vinegar, olive oil, minced garlic, salt, and pepper.
3. Brush the Portobello mushroom caps with the balsamic mixture.
4. Grill mushrooms for about 4-5 minutes per side until tender.
5. Split and toast slider buns until lightly browned.
6. Assemble sliders with grilled Portobello mushroom caps, vegan pesto, roasted red bell peppers, and baby spinach leaves.
7. Serve the Vegan Portobello Mushroom Sliders hot.
8. Enjoy!

4 servings

260 calories

30 mins

Vegan Buffalo Chickpea Sliders

Spicy buffalo chickpea sliders with cool vegan ranch!

Ingredients:

- 4 small vegan slider buns (check for vegan ingredients)
- 1 can chickpeas, drained and mashed
- 1/4 cup hot sauce (vegan)
- 2 tbsp vegan butter, melted
- 1/4 cup vegan ranch dressing
- 1/4 cup sliced celery
- 1/4 cup sliced red onion
- 1/4 cup baby spinach leaves
- Salt and pepper to taste

Directions

1. In a bowl, mix mashed chickpeas, hot sauce, melted vegan butter, salt, and pepper.
2. Split and toast slider buns until lightly browned.
3. Assemble sliders with buffalo chickpea mixture, sliced celery, sliced red onion, baby spinach leaves, and a drizzle of vegan ranch dressing.
4. Serve the Vegan Buffalo Chickpea Sliders with extra hot sauce if desired.
5. Enjoy!

Substitutions

None

4
servings

280
calories

35 mins

Vegan Hawaiian Sliders with Pineapple

Sweet and savory Hawaiian sliders with grilled pineapple!

Ingredients:

- 4 small vegan slider buns (check for vegan ingredients)
- 4 slices canned pineapple rings (in juice, not syrup)
- 4 vegan burger patties (store-bought or homemade)
- 1/4 cup vegan teriyaki sauce
- 1/4 cup vegan mayonnaise
- 1/4 cup shredded lettuce
- 1/4 cup sliced red onion
- Salt and pepper to taste

Directions

1. Preheat grill or grill pan over medium-high heat.
2. Grill pineapple rings for about 2-3 minutes per side until grill marks appear.
3. Grill vegan burger patties according to package instructions or your preferred recipe.
4. Split and toast slider buns until lightly browned.
5. In a bowl, mix vegan teriyaki sauce and vegan mayonnaise.
6. Assemble sliders with grilled pineapple rings, vegan burger patties, shredded lettuce, sliced red onion, and a drizzle of the teriyaki-mayo sauce.
7. Serve the Vegan Hawaiian Sliders with extra sauce if desired.
8. Enjoy!

Substitutions

None

4 servings

290 calories

35 mins

Vegan Smoky Tempeh Sliders

Smoky tempeh sliders with a touch of BBQ goodness!

Ingredients:

- 4 small vegan slider buns (check for vegan ingredients)
- 4 tempeh slices
- 1/4 cup BBQ sauce (vegan)
- 1/4 cup vegan coleslaw
- 1/4 cup sliced dill pickles
- 1/4 cup shredded lettuce
- 1/4 cup sliced red onion
- 2 tbsp olive oil
- Salt and pepper to taste

Substitutions

None

Directions

1. In a pan, heat olive oil over medium-high heat.
2. Sauté tempeh slices until golden brown on both sides.
3. Brush BBQ sauce onto the tempeh slices and cook for an additional 2-3 minutes.
4. Split and toast slider buns until lightly browned.
5. Assemble sliders with BBQ tempeh slices, vegan coleslaw, sliced dill pickles, shredded lettuce, sliced red onion, salt, and pepper.
6. Serve the Vegan Smoky Tempeh Sliders with extra BBQ sauce if desired.
7. Enjoy!

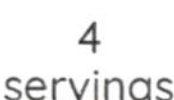
4 servings

270 calories

30 mins

Vegan Sloppy Joe Sliders

Classic sloppy joe sliders made with a vegan twist!

Ingredients:

- 4 small vegan slider buns (check for vegan ingredients)
- 1 cup vegan crumbles (soy or pea protein-based)
- 1/2 cup diced onion
- 1/2 cup diced green bell pepper
- 1/2 cup tomato sauce
- 2 tbsp tomato paste
- 2 tbsp ketchup (vegan)
- 1 tbsp brown sugar
- 1 tsp chili powder
- 1 tsp smoked paprika
- 1/2 tsp garlic powder
- Salt and pepper to taste

Directions

1. In a pan, sauté diced onion and diced green bell pepper until softened.
2. Add vegan crumbles and cook until heated through.
3. Stir in tomato sauce, tomato paste, ketchup, brown sugar, chili powder, smoked paprika, garlic powder, salt, and pepper.
4. Cook for an additional 5 minutes until the mixture thickens.
5. Split and toast slider buns until lightly browned.
6. Assemble sliders with the vegan sloppy joe mixture.
7. Serve the Vegan Sloppy Joe Sliders hot.
8. Enjoy!

Substitutions

None

4 servings | 260 calories | 35 mins

Vegan Falafel Sliders

Crispy falafel sliders with tahini sauce for a Mediterranean twist!

Ingredients:

- 4 small vegan slider buns (check for vegan ingredients)
- 4 vegan falafel patties (store-bought or homemade)
- 1/4 cup tahini sauce (vegan)
- 1/4 cup diced cucumber
- 1/4 cup diced tomato
- 1/4 cup shredded lettuce
- 1/4 cup sliced red onion
- Salt and pepper to taste

Directions

1. Cook vegan falafel patties according to package instructions or your preferred recipe.
2. Split and toast slider buns until lightly browned.
3. Assemble sliders with vegan falafel patties, tahini sauce, diced cucumber, diced tomato, shredded lettuce, sliced red onion, salt, and pepper.
4. Serve the Vegan Falafel Sliders with extra tahini sauce if desired.
5. Enjoy!

Substitutions

None

4
servings

280
calories

30 mins

Mini breakfast burritos filled with vegan goodness!

Vegan Mini Breakfast Burritos

Ingredients:

- 4 small flour tortillas (check for vegan ingredients)
- 1 cup vegan scrambled eggs
- 1/2 cup black beans, cooked and mashed
- 1/4 cup vegan cheddar cheese shreds
- 1/4 cup diced avocado
- 1/4 cup diced tomato
- 1/4 cup chopped fresh cilantro
- 2 tbsp salsa (check for vegan ingredients)
- Salt and pepper to taste

Substitutions

None

Directions

1. Warm flour tortillas in a dry skillet or microwave until pliable.
2. Assemble burritos with vegan scrambled eggs, mashed black beans, vegan cheddar cheese shreds, diced avocado, diced tomato, chopped fresh cilantro, salsa, salt, and pepper.
3. Roll up the burritos, folding in the sides as you go.
4. Serve the Vegan Mini Breakfast Burritos hot with extra salsa if desired.
5. Enjoy!

4 servings

290 calories

35 mins

Vegan Korean BBQ Sliders

Flavor-packed Korean BBQ sliders with a vegan twist!

Ingredients:

- 4 small vegan slider buns (check for vegan ingredients)
- 4 vegan burger patties (store-bought or homemade)
- 1/4 cup Korean BBQ sauce (vegan)
- 1/4 cup vegan kimchi
- 1/4 cup sliced cucumber
- 1/4 cup shredded lettuce
- 1/4 cup sliced green onion
- Salt and pepper to taste

Directions

1. Grill vegan burger patties according to package instructions or your preferred recipe.
2. Split and toast slider buns until lightly browned.
3. Assemble sliders with grilled vegan burger patties, Korean BBQ sauce, vegan kimchi, sliced cucumber, shredded lettuce, sliced green onion, salt, and pepper.
4. Serve the Vegan Korean BBQ Sliders with extra BBQ sauce if desired.
5. Enjoy!

Substitutions

None

4 servings | 250 calories | 25 mins

Vegan Caprese Sliders

Fresh Caprese sliders with vegan mozzarella and basil!

Ingredients:

- 4 small vegan slider buns (check for vegan ingredients)
- 4 vegan mozzarella slices
- 4 slices tomato
- 4 fresh basil leaves
- 2 tbsp balsamic glaze (check for vegan ingredients)
- Salt and pepper to taste

Directions

1. Split and toast slider buns until lightly browned.
2. Assemble sliders with vegan mozzarella slices, tomato slices, fresh basil leaves, a drizzle of balsamic glaze, salt, and pepper.
3. Serve the Vegan Caprese Sliders with extra balsamic glaze if desired.
4. Enjoy!

Substitutions

None

We have a small favor to ask

As we wrap up our culinary adventure through the pages of the Fast Food Vegan Cookbook: Satisfy Cravings, Stay Vegan - 100+ Plant-based Fast Food Inspired Recipes, I want to extend my deepest gratitude for taking this flavorful journey with me. Together, we've reimagined the world of fast food through a vegan lens, proving that indulgence and compassion can coexist in every bite.

Now, my fellow vegan food enthusiasts, I come to you with a heartfelt request—a request that has the power to make a world of difference to us, a dedicated team at a small but mighty publishing house. In the realm of cookbooks, reviews are the seasoning that transforms a dish from ordinary to extraordinary. They are as elusive as the perfect French fry, yet they are the lifeblood of our creative spirit.

If these recipes have allowed you to satisfy your cravings while staying true to your vegan values, if they've brought the thrill of fast food into your plant-based kitchen, I would be immensely grateful if you could spare a moment. Please return to the app or platform where you acquired this book, and there you'll find a review button waiting for your touch. A star rating and a brief sentence sharing your thoughts would be the equivalent of a standing ovation in the culinary world.

You see, being a small publisher, every review is a beacon of hope that guides us forward. Your words can inspire others to embrace the joy of vegan fast food, one delectable dish at a time.

Rest assured, every review is not just welcomed but cherished. We understand that, even in the finest kitchens, the most skilled chefs may occasionally make a minor misstep. If you happen to spot any such hiccup along the way, please know that we've poured our hearts and souls into this cookbook. We're only human, and in the world of cooking, sometimes a dash of imperfection is part of the magic.

From the bottom of our hearts, thank you for choosing the Fast Food Vegan Cookbook, and thank you in advance for considering leaving a review. Your support fuels our passion for creating more delicious, compassionate, and satisfying vegan experiences. Until we meet again on the pages of another cookbook, may your plant-based fast food adventures be filled with flavor, joy, and a sense of culinary revolution.

www.ingramcontent.com/pod-product-compliance
Ingram Content Group UK Ltd.
Pitfield, Milton Keynes, MK11 3LW, UK
UKRC032233290726
14090UKWH00009B/495